A SENSE OF COMFORT
For You And Your Loved Ones

by
Frank L. Nelson

First published by Dog Ear Publishing
4010 W. 86th Street, Ste H
Indianapolis, IN 46268
www.dogearpublishing.net

ISBN: 978-1-4575-1757-0

This paper is printed on acid free paper.
Printed in the United States of America

ACKNOWLEDGEMENTS

I would first like to thank God, who has been my constant companion, and who has given me strength through good and difficult times. Through Him all things are possible.

I dedicate this book to my wonderful wife, Renee, for her love, unwavering support and belief in my ability to make a positive difference in the lives of others, and for her endless hours of editing help.

I also want to acknowledge and thank the following people who provided invaluable reviews and commentaries: Ed O'Hara, Steve and Maggie Meigs, Reg Miller, Bob Gerstemeier, and Gary Altman.

A SENSE OF COMFORT
For You And Your Loved Ones

TABLE OF CONTENTS

PART I - GETTING PREPARED

PART II - GOING INTO ACTION

PART III - OTHER THINGS YOU NEED TO KNOW

A SENSE OF COMFORT
For You And Your Loved Ones

INTRODUCTION

Although it is difficult to think about, death and disability don't always give us time to prepare. One spouse or partner may suddenly die, or both could die in a tragic accident leaving grief stricken family members to manage the many challenges of settling financial affairs. Though completing Part I of this workbook may be somewhat tedious, doing so is a gift of love; it will keep on giving even when you are unable to give any more.

In the event of a death or incapacitation, it can be emotionally overwhelming for loved ones or others to step in and take appropriate action in a timely manner. The purpose of this workbook is three-fold:

- to help you organize your personal affairs in case you die or become incapacitated;
- to provide important information and answers to questions that may arise for those you've chosen to tend to your affairs; and
- to give yourself a sense of comfort now knowing your loved ones will be greatly comforted and helped during a time of loss and confusion.

Also included is a glossary of terms that are used throughout the workbook, as well as other terms that might be of use.

Advanced planning and organization of your affairs is imperative to ensure that your wishes are carried out if you should die or become incapacitated. We can never know for sure when decisions will have to be made on our behalf, so we must decide who will make those decisions for us and provide instructions to guide them. Being organized makes it easier for others to act in your best interest. This workbook is designed to help you provide that guidance, and give you and your loved ones a sense of comfort in difficult times.

Because some information might change over time, if you have purchased a printed copy of this workbook, you have permission to make copies of those pages that could potentially change for your own personal use.

Frank L. Nelson, LFACHE, RTRP, CFP[®]

A word about SECURITY before we get started…

In the same way that you protect your electronic information or any other valuables, be sure to safeguard the information you compile on these pages. Keep the workbook in a safe and private place. Only you and those you trust should be aware of and have access to it.

PART I

GETTING PREPARED

* * * * * *   * * * * * *   * * * * * *

While none of us want to think about the possibility of becoming incapacitated or of our inevitable death, it is imperative that we provide our loved ones with the information they need to handle a myriad of required actions. Because our families will be stressed enough, it is important not to leave them in the dark, digging to find important documents and information.

Here in Part I of the workbook, you'll fill out some detailed forms to record personal information that your loved ones may need in the event of your incapacitation or death. Part II outlines the steps to accomplish. Please use the 'Additional Information' sections as a continuation of the information provided previously and/or simply to include additional information/instructions.

Completing these forms may seem daunting, however it needn't be completed in one sitting. You might consider spreading the task over a period of days. Once you are finished, you'll feel relieved, knowing that when the time comes, your loved ones will be grateful for your thoroughness.

The forms should be reviewed at least annually, or whenever significant changes occur.

* * * * * *   * * * * * *   * * * * * *

A SENSE OF COMFORT
For You And Your Loved Ones

* * * * * *   * * * * * *   * * * * * *

1. PERSONAL INFORMATION - YOU

NAME: ____   ___________________

First / Middle / Last   Social Security Number

ADDRESS:____

Street/City/State/Zip

P.O. BOX:_________________________________ DRIVERS LICENSE #_______________

Box # / City / State / Zip

_____________________________________ ________________________________

Home Telephone   Cell Telephone

EMAIL(S):____

Address / User Name / Password

____

Address / User Name / Password

BIRTH INFO:

_____ / _____ / _____ / _________________________________   ___________________

Mo Day Year   City   State

☐ Birth Certificate - Additional copies of Birth Certificate are located:_________________

____

☐ Marriage Certificates / Divorce Decrees - Originals and other copies of all marriage certificates and divorce decrees are located:_______________________________

____

KEYS (check all that you carry)

☐HOUSE ☐OFFICE ☐HOME SAFE ☐SAFE/BANK DEPOSIT BOX ☐P.O. BOX ☐STORAGE SHED
☐CAR ☐RV ☐VACATION / 2ND HOME ☐STORAGE RENTAL UNIT ☐BOAT ☐MOTORCYCLE
☐OTHER____

HOME SAFE COMBINATION:________________ My keys and/or duplicates are located:

____

EMPLOYMENT
☐ Unemployed ☐Retired ☐Self-Employed (List business address/PO Box below if applicable)

☐ Employed

____

Name of Employer / Company

10

A SENSE OF COMFORT
For You And Your Loved Ones

____   ___________________
Work Address   Work Telephone

____
Name / Phone Number of Contact Person

If Self-Employed:
☐Sole Proprietor   ☐LLC   ☐Other Do You Have A Business Partner? ☐Yes ☐No

Business Partner Contact Information (If applicable):_______________________
                                                    Name

____   ___________________________
              Address   Telephone

____
Business Partner Access Information (User Name(s), Password(s), etc.)

____   ___________________________
Location of Office Keys (If Applicable)   Office Safe Combination

Business Account(s):__________________________   ___________________________
                    Type of Account   Account Number

_________________________________   ___________________________________
        Name of Bank   Address

____
        Online Access Information (User Name, Password, etc.)

Business Bank / Safe Deposit Box ☐No ☐Yes If Yes, key location:________________

____

Others To Be Notified (*Employees, Creditors, Vendors, Business Accountant, Property Manager, etc.*):

____   ___________________________
        Name / Business Relationship   Telephone

____   ___________________________
        Name / Business Relationship   Telephone

____   ___________________________
        Name / Business Relationship   Telephone

____   ___________________________
        Name / Business Relationship   Telephone

____   ___________________________
        Name / Business Relationship   Telephone

____   ___________________________
        Name / Business Relationship   Telephone

A SENSE OF COMFORT
For You And Your Loved Ones

* * * * * *   * * * * * *   * * * * * *

1-A. PERSONAL INFORMATION - YOUR SPOUSE

NAME: ____   __________________

First / Middle / Last

Social Security Number

ADDRESS:____

Street/City/State/Zip

P.O. BOX:_________________________________ DRIVERS LICENSE #_______________

Box # / City / State / Zip

_______________________________   _______________________________

Home Telephone   Cell Telephone

EMAIL(S):____

Address / User Name / Password

____

Address / User Name / Password

BIRTH INFO:

____ / ____ / ______ / ________________________   _______________________

Mo   Day   Year   City   State

☐ Birth Certificate - Additional copies of Birth Certificate are located:_______________

____

☐ Marriage Certificates / Divorce Decrees - Originals and other copies of all marriage certificates and divorce decrees are located:_______________________

____

KEYS (check all that you carry)

☐HOUSE ☐OFFICE ☐HOME SAFE ☐SAFE/BANK DEPOSIT BOX ☐P.O. BOX ☐STORAGE SHED
☐CAR ☐RV ☐VACATION / 2ND HOME ☐STORAGE RENTAL UNIT ☐BOAT ☐MOTORCYCLE
☐OTHER____

HOME SAFE COMBINATION:_________________ My keys and/or duplicates are located:

____

EMPLOYMENT

☐ Unemployed   ☐Retired   ☐Self-Employed (List business address/PO Box below if applicable)   ☐ Employed

____

Name of Employer / Company

_______________________________   _______________________

Work Address   Work Telephone

A SENSE OF COMFORT
For You And Your Loved Ones

Name / Phone Number of Contact Person

If Self-Employed:
□Sole Proprietor   □LLC   □Other   Do You Have A Business Partner? □Yes □No

Business Partner Contact Information (If applicable):_______________________
Name

____   ______________________
Address   Telephone

____
Business Partner Access Information (User Name(s), Password(s), etc.)

______________________________________   ___________________________
Location of Office Keys (If Applicable)   Combination To Office Safe

Business Account(s):_______________________   _____________________
Type of Account   Account Number

_________________________   ________________________________
Name of Bank   Address

____
Online Access Information (User Name, Password, etc.)

Business Bank / Safe Deposit Box □No □Yes If Yes, key location:_____________

____

Others To Be Notified (*Employees, Creditors, Vendors, Business Accountant, Property Manager, etc.):*

____   ______________________
Name / Business Relationship   Telephone

____   ______________________
Name / Business Relationship   Telephone

____   ______________________
Name / Business Relationship   Telephone

____   ______________________
Name / Business Relationship   Telephone

____   ______________________
Name / Business Relationship   Telephone

____   ______________________
Name / Business Relationship   Telephone

ADDITIONAL INFORMATION FOR THIS SECTION:

* * * * * *   * * * * * *   * * * * * *

2. IMPORTANT ITEMS / PAPERS

Having a well thought out and executed estate plan ensures your desires are accomplished. Additionally, a well thought out and functioning estate plan can be one of the best gifts a person can give to a loved one or parents can give to their children. The ability to quickly and efficiently take care of all the details for someone's estate can be a great relief to surviving spouses and children when they are still grieving from the loss of a family member. If you do not have a comprehensive estate plan your financial advisor can assist you and guide you to an estate planning attorney to complete the necessary estate documents. If you do not have a financial advisor, in Part III you'll find a section on how to choose a financial advisor. Make sure that you retain the original copies of the estate documents.

Check all that apply:

☐ LAST WILL AND TESTAMENT ☐ LIVING WILL ☐ ETHICAL WILL ☐ TRUST ☐ BEQUESTS
☐ MEDICAL DIRECTIVE ☐ SPECIAL POWER OF ATTORNEY ☐ GUARDIANSHIP ☐ HOME SAFE
☐ STORAGE UNIT ☐ SAFE/ SAFE DEPOSIT KEY ☐ POST OFFICE BOX KEY ☐ YOUR GUARDIAN
☐ DURABLE GENERAL FINANCIAL POWER OF ATTORNEY (DGFPoA)
☐ BANK, BROKERAGE, OR OTHER FINANCIAL INSTITUTION'S POWER OF ATTORNEY

Originals and other copies of these documents are located:__________________________

____

____

Location of home safe / storage unit(s) (if applicable):____________________________

____

Home Safe / Lock Combination(s):____

____

Name(s) of person(s) with access to home safe and/or storage units:

____ Phone:__________________________

____ Phone:__________________________

____ Phone:__________________________

* * * * * *   * * * * * *   * * * * * *

3. HEALTH CARE DIRECTIVES (In case of incapacitation)

If the following information is already detailed in your estate plan documents, simply indicate next to each item where the information can be found. If not or if you do not have an estate plan, it is imperative that you seek a financial advisor and/or an estate planning attorney to assist you in developing a comprehensive estate plan.

Primary person given Durable General Financial Power of Attorney:

____   _______________________
Name   Phone

____
Address

Secondary person given Durable General Financial Power of Attorney:

____   _______________________
Name   Phone

____
Address

Primary person given Power of Attorney for medical decisions:

____   _______________________
Name   Phone

____
Address

Secondary person given Power of Attorney for medical decisions:

____   _______________________
Name   Phone

____
Address

HOW YOU WISH TO BE CARED FOR*

It should be noted that the following health care directives, should you become incapacitated, are not binding on your physicians, family or any agent named in your Advanced Medical Directive. They are simply an expression of your wishes.

Diagnostic Tests: Under what circumstances, if any, would you **not** consent to diagnostic tests ordered by your physician (e.g., if the test were not clearly related to your treatment; if your medical situation was hopeless unless the tests would help you psychologically or benefit someone else)?____

____

____

A SENSE OF COMFORT
For You And Your Loved Ones

Surgery: Under what circumstances, if any, would you **not** consent to surgery (e.g., if it were not to restore your health or not free you from unbearable pain)? ________________________

____

____

Hospital or home care: If your death is not sudden, but imminent, where would you prefer to die (home, hospital, or support care facility such as hospice)?________________________

____

____

Cardio-pulmonary resuscitation (CPR): Under what circumstances would you **not** consent to CPR (e.g., if your heart stopped beating and there was no reasonable expectation of your returning to unaided functioning)?____

____

____

Amputation: Under what circumstance would you consent to amputation (e.g., to prolong your life; if limb is already substantially severed and your life is threatened by infection)?________________________

____

____

Naso-gastric feeding: Will you accept feeding through a naso-gastric tube if necessary? Or would you prefer to be fed intravenously or otherwise?________________________________

____

____

Surgically emplaced feeding tubes: Under what circumstances would you consent to surgically emplaced feeding tubes (in stomach or intestines)?____________________________________

____

____

Pain relief: Under what circumstances would you **not** want pain relief?________________

____

____

Mechanical life support: Under what circumstances would you **not** consent to or **not** want to be removed from mechanical life support?____

____

____

No brain activity: In the absence of brain activity, do you wish to be kept alive by artificial means?____

Terminal, Irreversible Illness: If your condition is terminal/irreversible, under what circumstances would you consent to aggressive medical or surgical procedures in an effort to extend your life?____

____

____

Financial burden of life sustaining support: Should your treatment from mechanical life support, no brain activity, or terminal/irreversible illness becomes a financial burden to your family, do you consent to being removed from mechanical life support?___________________________

____

Loss of cognitive ability (knowing, perceiving, and understanding things): Under what circumstances would you **not** want to be treated for life-threatening conditions if you lost your ability to know, perceive, or understand things?____

____

____

Organ Donation When You Die: Do you wish to donate any part of your body when you die? If so, what parts do you authorize your representative to donate for transplanting in another human being (e.g., heart, kidneys, lungs, liver, skin, corneas, pancreas, etc)?___________________________

____

____

Do you have a specific person or institution to whom you wish to donate your organs and/or body parts? If so, provide details.____

____

____

4. EXECUTOR / EXECUTRIX, TRUSTEE or PERSONAL REPRESENTATIVE, GUARDIAN

If you have a WILL or TRUST, list the following information:

TRUSTEE:_______________________________   ___________________
Name Phone

_______________________________   ___________________
Address Email

18

A SENSE OF COMFORT
For You And Your Loved Ones

SUCCESSOR
TRUSTEE: ___________________________________   ___________________________
                        Name   Phone

___________________________________   ___________________________
            Address   Email

EXECUTOR /
EXECUTRIX: __________________________________   ___________________________
                        Name   Phone

___________________________________   ___________________________
            Address   Email

PERSONAL
REPRESENTATIVE: ______________________________   ___________________________
                            Name   Phone

___________________________________   ___________________________
            Address   Email

If someone has been appointed as your Guardian, list the following information:

___________________________________   ___________________________
         Guardian's Name   Phone

___________________________________   ___________________________
            Address   Email

ADDITIONAL INFORMATION FOR THIS SECTION:

____

____

____

____

____

____

____

____

____

* * * * * *   * * * * * *   * * * * * *

5. MINOR CHILDREN

List the names and ages of your minor children if applicable:

Name	Age	Social Security Number

Name	Age	Social Security Number

Name	Age	Social Security Number

Important health information:

GUARDIAN: List information about the person(s) you have designated as guardian(s) for your minor child(ren)*

Name of Guardian #1	Social Security Number	Phone Number

Address		Email Address

Name of Guardian #2	Social Security Number	Phone Number

Address		Email Address

**Be certain that the person you name as Guardian of your child(ren) is able and willing to care for them.*

* * * * * *   * * * * * *   * * * * * *

Are you the guardian of any minor children, or of any adult? ☐Yes ☐No
If yes, please specify who:

1.

Name	Age	Phone

Address

A SENSE OF COMFORT
For You And Your Loved Ones

2.____ ______ ____________
    Name   Age   Phone

____
    Address

3.____ ______ ____________
    Name   Age   Phone

____
    Address

* * * * * *   * * * * * *   * * * * * *

Are you the custodian of any minor children's accounts (UGMA/UTMA)? If yes:

1.____ ______ ____________
    Name of minor   Age   Phone

____
    Address

____ _____________________________
    Name of Bank / Broker/ Company / Plan   Name of contact person

____ _____________________________
                  Address   Phone

____ _____________________________
         Type of Investment   Account Number

______________________________ ________________________ / ________________
      Web site address   LOGIN INFO: User ID   Password

2.____ ______ ____________
    Name of minor   Age   Phone

____
    Address

____ _____________________________
    Name of Bank / Broker/ Company / Plan   Name of contact person

____ _____________________________
                  Address   Phone

____ _____________________________
         Type of Investment   Account Number

______________________________ ________________________ / ________________
      Web site address   LOGIN INFO: User ID   Password

3.____ ______ ____________
    Name of minor   Age   Phone

A SENSE OF COMFORT
For You And Your Loved Ones

____
Address

_______________________________   ______________________________
Name of Bank / Broker/ Company / Plan   Name of contact person

_______________________________   ______________________________
Address   Phone

_______________________________   ______________________________
Type of Investment   Account Number

_______________________   _________________ / ________________
Web site address   LOGIN INFO: User ID   Password

* * * * * *   * * * * * *   * * * * * *

6. ADULT CHILDREN and/or OTHER INTENDED BENEFICIARIES

1.___________________________________   ______________________
                      Name   Telephone

____
                      Address

2.___________________________________   ______________________
                      Name   Telephone

____
                      Address

3.___________________________________   ______________________
                      Name   Telephone

____
                      Address

4.___________________________________   ______________________
                      Name   Telephone

____
                      Address

5.___________________________________   ______________________
                      Name   Telephone

____
                      Address

6.___________________________________   ______________________
                      Name   Telephone

____
                      Address

A SENSE OF COMFORT
For You And Your Loved Ones

ADDITIONAL INFORMATION FOR THIS SECTION:

A SENSE OF COMFORT
For You And Your Loved Ones

* * * * * *   * * * * * *   * * * * * *

7. PETS

☐Cat ☐Dog ☐Bird
☐Other:____

____
Name   Breed   Color   Age

Medications:____

☐Cat ☐Dog ☐Bird
☐Other:____

____
Name   Breed   Color   Age

Medications:____

VETERINARIAN___________________________________ _______________
Name   Phone

PET INSURANCE:_________________________________ _______________
Name of Insurance   Phone

List information about the person(s) you designate to care for your pet(s)*

______________________________ ______________________________
Name   Phone

______________________________ ______________________________
Address   Email Address

______________________________ ______________________________
Name   Phone

______________________________ ______________________________
Address   Email Address

**Be certain that the person you name as Guardian of your pet(s) is able and willing to care for them.*

* * * * * *   * * * * * *   * * * * * *

8. EMERGENCY CONTACT(S)

Who should be notified in the event of your hospitalization or death?

☐ I have an attorney:________________________________ _______________
Name   Phone

______________________________ ______________________________
Address   Email Address

A SENSE OF COMFORT
For You And Your Loved Ones

Others:

1. ____   ________________________
              Name   Phone

____   ________________________
              Address   Email Address

2. ____   ________________________
              Name   Phone

____   ________________________
              Address   Email Address

3. ____   ________________________
              Name   Phone

____   ________________________
              Address   Email Address

4. ____   ________________________
              Name   Phone

____   ________________________
              Address   Email Address

5. ____   ________________________
              Name   Phone

____   ________________________
              Address   Email Address

6. ____   ________________________
              Name   Phone

____   ________________________
              Address   Email Address

7. ____   ________________________
              Name   Phone

____   ________________________
              Address   Email Address

8. ____   ________________________
              Name   Phone

____   ________________________
              Address   Email Address

ADDITIONAL INFORMATION FOR THIS SECTION:

A SENSE OF COMFORT
For You And Your Loved Ones

* * * * * *   * * * * * *   * * * * * *

9. EMERGENCY MEDICAL INFORMATION

Name of Primary Care Physician	Phone
Specialist Physician's Name / Specialty	Phone
Specialist Physician's Name / Specialty	Phone
Name of Dentist	Phone

MEDICAL CONDITIONS (INCLUDING ALLERGIES):

____

____

____

MEDICATIONS:

Medication 1	For what condition	Prescriber's Name	Strength / Dose
Medication 2	For what condition	Prescriber's Name	Strength / Dose
Medication 3	For what condition	Prescriber's Name	Strength / Dose
Medication 4	For what condition	Prescriber's Name	Strength / Dose
Medication 5	For what condition	Prescriber's Name	Strength / Dose

PHARMACY:____

Name / Location / Phone# of local Pharmacy used to obtain medications

MAIL-ORDER
PHARMACY:____

Name / Phone# of mail-order Pharmacy used to obtain medications

____

Online Account Access Information (Website, Account #, User Name, Password, etc.)

LOCATION OF:

Medical Records	Dental Records
Vaccination Records	Other

A SENSE OF COMFORT
For You And Your Loved Ones

MEDICAL INSURANCE:

_____________________________________ _____________________________________
Name of Primary Policy Holder   Policy Number

_____________________________________ _____________________________________
Primary Insurance Company Name   Phone

_____________________________________ _____________________________________
Name of Secondary Policy Holder   Policy Number

_____________________________________ _____________________________________
Secondary Insurance Company Name   Phone

INSURANCE CARDS ARE LOCATED:_________________________________

* * * * * *   * * * * * *   * * * * * *

ADDITIONAL INFORMATION FOR THIS SECTION:

____

____

____

____

____

____

____

____

____

____

____

____

____

* * * * * *   * * * * * *   * * * * * *

10. FUNERAL ARRANGEMENTS

This information should be discussed ahead of time with your spouse, next of kin, and/or the executor/executrix of your estate.

I wish to have/be:☐Cremated ☐My Organs Donated ☐An Open Casket Viewing   ☐A Private, Family-Only Funeral   ☐A Closed Casket Wake ☐A Memorial Service ☐A Grave-side Service ☐ OTHER: ____

____

☐ I have pre-arranged my services (*Include copies of detailed paperwork*) Original paperwork is located: ____

FUNERAL HOME: ____

_______________________________________   _______________________________
Address   Phone

CEMETARY:_________________________________   _______________________________
Name   Phone

_______________________________________   _______________________________
Address   Plot Number

PLACE OF WORSHIP:____

PASTOR / PRIEST / RABBI, etc:_________________________   _______________________
Name   Phone

In the event of my death, notify the following people:

_______________________   _______________________   _______________________
Name 1   Relationship   Phone

_______________________   _______________________   _______________________
Name 2   Relationship   Phone

_______________________   _______________________   _______________________
Name 3   Relationship   Phone

_______________________   _______________________   _______________________
Name 4   Relationship   Phone

_______________________   _______________________   _______________________
Name 5   Relationship   Phone

_______________________   _______________________   _______________________
Name 6   Relationship   Phone

Name 7	Relationship	Phone
Name 8	Relationship	Phone
Name 9	Relationship	Phone
Name 10	Relationship	Phone

PERSONAL EFFECTS:

In the event of your death, specify what should be done with your personal effects (*Given to whom, what charities, sold, donated, etc.*):

____

____

____

____

____

____

____

____

____

____

____

____

ADDITIONAL INFORMATION FOR THIS SECTION:

11. PROPERTY

MORTGAGE: ________________________________ ________________________
Name of Lender   Phone

____ ________________________
Lender Address   Loan Number

2ND MORTGAGE: ______________________________ ________________________
Name of Lender   Phone

____ ________________________
Lender Address   Loan Number

REVERSE MORTGAGE:__________________________ ________________________
Name of Lender   Phone

____ ________________________
Lender Address   Loan Number

HOME EQUITY LINE OF CREDIT:__________________ ________________________
Name of Lender   Phone

____ ________________________
Lender Address   Loan Number

☐DEED - Original and other copies are located:__________________________

RENTAL(S) ☐ RENTAL AGREEMENT - If you rent your home, list the following:

____ ________________________
Landlord's Name   Phone

OTHER REAL ESTATE: List details of other real estate including location(s), location of Deeds, lender information and loan number(s):

____

____

RENTAL
PROPERTY:____
Location Address

____
Property Management Company (If any)

____
Mortgage Company

Who Should Be Notified:____
(Tenants, Property Manager, etc.)

____

AUTOMOBILES:

1. ______________________________ ______________________________ ______________________________
      Make   Model   License Plate Number

LOCATION OF TITLE:____

☐OWN ☐OWE ☐ LEASE ______________________________ ______________________________
      Name of Lender / Leasing Agent   Phone

______________________________ ______________________________
    Lender / Lessor Address   Loan Number

2. ______________________________ ______________________________ ______________________________
      Make   Model   License Plate Number

LOCATION OF TITLE:____

☐OWN ☐OWE ☐ LEASE ______________________________ ______________________________
      Name of Lender / Leasing Agent   Phone

______________________________ ______________________________
    Lender / Lessor Address   Loan Number

3. ______________________________ ______________________________ ______________________________
      Make   Model   License Plate Number

LOCATION OF TITLE:____

☐OWN ☐OWE ☐ LEASE ______________________________ ______________________________
      Name of Lender / Leasing Agent   Phone

______________________________ ______________________________
    Lender / Lessor Address   Loan Number

4. ______________________________ ______________________________ ______________________________
      Make   Model   License Plate Number

LOCATION OF TITLE:____

☐OWN ☐OWE ☐ LEASE ______________________________ ______________________________
      Name of Lender / Leasing Agent   Phone

______________________________ ______________________________
    Lender / Lessor Address   Loan Number

* * * * *   * * * * * *   * * * * * *

ADDITIONAL INFORMATION FOR THIS SECTION:

____

____

12. INSURANCE - Dental

_______________________________________   _______________________________________
Insurance Company   Insurance Agent

____
Insurance Company Address

_______________________________________   _______________________________________
Policy Number   Phone Number

POLICY LOCATED:_______________________________________

INSURANCE - Disability

_______________________________________   _______________________________________
Insurance Company   Insurance Agent

____
Insurance Company Address

_______________________________________   _______________________________________
Policy Number   Phone Number

POLICY LOCATED:

____

INSURANCE - Long Term Care

_______________________________________   _______________________________________
Insurance Company   Insurance Agent

____
Insurance Company Address

_______________________________________   _______________________________________
Policy Number   Phone Number

POLICY LOCATED: _______________________________________

INSURANCE - Life

_______________________________________   _______________________________________
Insurance Company   Insurance Agent

_______________________________________   _______________________________________
Insurance Company Address   Phone

_______________________________   _______________________   _______________________
Type of Insurance   Policy Number   Insurance Amount

POLICY LOCATED: _______________________________________

_______________________________________   _______________________________________
Name of Primary Beneficiary   Relationship

A SENSE OF COMFORT
For You And Your Loved Ones

____   _______________________
Primary Beneficiary Address   Phone

____   _______________________
Name of Secondary Beneficiary   Relationship

____   _______________________
Second Beneficiary Address   Phone

How would you like the proceeds of the policy to be used?________________________

____

POLICY #2 _______________________________   _______________________________
                Insurance Company   Insurance Agent

____   _______________________
Insurance Company Address   Phone

____________________________   _________________   _______________________
Type of Insurance   Policy Number   Insurance Amount

POLICY LOCATED: ____

____   _______________________________
Name of Primary Beneficiary   Relationship

____   _______________________________
Primary Beneficiary Address   Phone

____   _______________________________
Name of Secondary Beneficiary   Relationship

____   _______________________________
Second Beneficiary Address   Phone

How would you like the proceeds of the policy to be used?________________________

____

* * * * * *   * * * * * *   * * * * * *

INSURANCE - Home Owners

____   _______________________________
Insurance Company   Insurance Agent

____   _______________________________
Insurance Company Address   Phone

_________________________________   _______________________________________
Policy Number   Policy Location

A SENSE OF COMFORT
For You And Your Loved Ones

* * * * * *　　* * * * * *　　* * * * * *

INSURANCE - Umbrella

_______________________________   _______________________________
Insurance Company   Insurance Agent

____
Insurance Company Address

_______________________________   _______________________________
Policy Number   Phone Number

POLICY LOCATED: ____

* * * * * *　　* * * * * *　　* * * * * *

INSURANCE - Auto

_______________________________   _______________________________
Insurance Company   Insurance Agent

____
Insurance Company Address

_______________________________   _______________________________
Policy Number   Phone Number

POLICY LOCATED: ____

* * * * * *　　* * * * * *　　* * * * * *

INSURANCE - Boat

_______________________________   _______________________________
Insurance Company   Insurance Agent

____
Insurance Company Address

_______________________________   _______________________________
Policy Number   Phone Number

POLICY LOCATED: ____

* * * * * *　　* * * * * *　　* * * * * *

INSURANCE - Airplane

_______________________________   _______________________________
Insurance Company   Insurance Agent

____
Insurance Company Address

_______________________________   _______________________________
Policy Number   Phone Number

POLICY LOCATED: ____

A SENSE OF COMFORT
For You And Your Loved Ones

ADDITIONAL INFORMATION FOR THIS SECTION:

13. FINANCES - Different institutions have different requirements/policies regarding the handling of your financial accounts by someone other than yourself. Some companies will accept a power of attorney from your chosen representative, while others require the use of their own specific forms. *It is important that you check with each institution to ensure that you have the correct, complete and up-to-date paperwork on file in the event of an emergency.*

LEGAL AGENT (The person legally appointed to handle your financial affairs under the Durable Financial Power of Attorney, Guardianship, or your financial institution's Specific Power of Attorney):

Name	Phone
Address	Email

FINANCIAL ADVISOR:

Name	Phone
Address	Email

ACCOUNTANT:

Name	Phone
Address	Email

PERSONAL COMPUTER / LAPTOP / IPAD: Provide User Name and Password and/or any other information necessary to access information:

LIST PERSONS WITH ACCESS TO: Your Safe Deposit Box, Home Safe, Storage Unit, etc.

____ Phone: ____________________

____ Phone: ____________________

____ Phone: ____________________

____ Phone: ____________________

13-A. Debt: Credit / Debit Cards

1. ________________________   ________________________________   ________________
Type (VISA, MC, SEARS, etc.)   Account Number   Expiration Date

________________________   ________________________________   ________________
Credit Card Company   Phone

2. ________________________   ________________________________   ________________
Type (VISA, MC, SEARS, etc.)   Account Number   Expiration Date

____   _______________________
Credit Card Company   Phone

3. ______________________ ________________________ ______________________
Type (VISA, MC, SEARS, ETC.)   Account Number   Expiration Date

____   _______________________
Credit Card Company   Phone

Debt - Other *(Mortgage Line of Credit, Auto Loan, Student Loans...)*

1. _________________________________ ________________ __________________
   Name of company or person owed   Amount you owe   Phone

_______________________________________ ___________________________________
Address   Account Number

2. _________________________________ ________________ __________________
   Name of company or person owed   Amount you owe   Phone

_______________________________________ ___________________________________
Address   Account Number

3. _________________________________ ________________ __________________
   Name of company or person owed   Amount you owe   Phone

_______________________________________ ___________________________________
Address   Account Number

Debts Owed To You

_________________________________ ________________ __________________
Name of person who owes you   Amount owed to you   Phone

DOCUMENTS OF PROOF ARE LOCATED:____

_________________________________ ________________ __________________
Name of person who owes you   Amount owed to you   Phone

DOCUMENTS OF PROOF ARE LOCATED:____

* * * * * *   * * * * * *   * * * * * *

13-B. Investments

Do you have investments in: single☐ or joint☐ accounts? If so, with whom are your accounts located?: Brokers☐ Banks☐ Mutual Fund Companies☐ Dividend Reinvestment Plans☐ Annuities☐ Provide pertinent information for all the investments you have:

1. ___________________________________ ___________________________________
   Name of Bank / Broker/ Company / Plan   Name of contact person

_______________________________________ ___________________________________
Address   Phone

A SENSE OF COMFORT
For You And Your Loved Ones

____   ___________________________
Type of Investment   Account Number

____
Name(s) of Joint Account Holder(s)

____   _________/_________________
Web site address   LOGIN INFO: User ID / Password

2. ____   ___________________________
Name of Bank / Broker/ Company / Plan   Name of contact person

____   ___________________________
Address   Phone

____   ___________________________
Type of Investment   Account Number

____
Name(s) of Joint Account Holder(s)

____   _________/_________________
Web site address   LOGIN INFO: User ID / Password

3. ____   ___________________________
Name of Bank / Broker/ Company / Plan   Name of contact person

____   ___________________________
Address   Phone

____   ___________________________
Type of Investment   Account Number

____
Name(s) of Joint Account Holder(s)

____   _________/_________________
Web site address   LOGIN INFO: User ID / Password

4. ____   ___________________________
Name of Bank / Broker/ Company / Plan   Name of contact person

____   ___________________________
Address   Phone

____   ___________________________
Type of Investment   Account Number

____
Name(s) of Joint Account Holder(s)

____   _________/_________________
Web site address   LOGIN INFO: User ID / Password

5. ____   ___________________________
Name of Bank / Broker/ Company / Plan   Name of contact person

____   ___________________________
Address   Phone

A SENSE OF COMFORT
For You And Your Loved Ones

Type of Investment	Account Number

Name(s) of Joint Account Holder(s)

Web site address	/
	LOGIN INFO: User ID / Password

6. _______________________________

Name of Bank / Broker/ Company / Plan	Name of contact person

Address	Phone

Type of Investment	Account Number

Name(s) of Joint Account Holder(s)

	/
Web site address	LOGIN INFO: User ID / Password

Do you have investment and/or other financial information in folders on your computer? ☐YES ☐ NO   If yes, where is the detailed information located on your computer, and how do you access it?_______________________________

____

If you have single bank accounts, are they: ☐Payable on Death (POD) or ☐Transfer on Death (TOD)? Who is the payee:_______________________________ _______________________________

Name	Phone

Address	Email Address

Check all of the following that you have:

☐Government Savings or Corporate/Municipal bonds   Where are they located? _____________

____

☐Certificates of Deposit   Where are they located?_______________________________

____

CD#1 _______________________________   _______________________________

Financial Institution	Account Number

Phone #	Web Site Address	User ID / Password

CD#2 _______________________________   _______________________________

Financial Institution	Account Number

Phone #	Web Site Address	User ID / Password

A SENSE OF COMFORT
For You And Your Loved Ones

CD#3 ____   _______________________________
Financial Institution   Account Number

__________________   __________________________   _______________________________
Phone #   Web Site Address   User ID / Password

CD#4 ____   _______________________________
Financial Institution   Account Number

__________________   __________________________   _______________________________
Phone #   Web Site Address   User ID / Password

CD#5 ____   _______________________________
Financial Institution   Account Number

__________________   __________________________   _______________________________
Phone #   Web Site Address   User ID / Password

☐ Stock Certificates   Where are they located?

____

____

How do you keep track of your investments (e.g., folders with account statements, spreadsheets, other computer software, online)? ____

____

Do you have investment and/or other financial information in folders on your computer? ☐ Yes ☐ No   If yes, where is this detailed information located on your computer, and how do you access it? ____

____

If you maintain investment spreadsheets, where are they and how are they updated? ___________

____

Do you maintain information on investments in folders/notebooks in your home? ☐ Yes ☐ No

If yes, which investments, and where are these folders/notebooks located? _________________

____

Do you have a Safe Deposit Box? ☐ Yes ☐ No If yes, at which bank, and where is the key located? ____

____
Address of Bank Branch

Safe Deposit key location: ____

* * * * * *   * * * * * *   * * * * * *

A SENSE OF COMFORT
For You And Your Loved Ones

ADDITIONAL INFORMATION FOR THIS SECTION:

A SENSE OF COMFORT
For You And Your Loved Ones

* * * * * *   * * * * * *   * * * * * *

14. RETIREMENT

Do you have any of the following: Pension Plan☐   401K☐   403B☐   457 Plan☐   Roth
IRA☐ Traditional IRA☐   TSP☐   SEP IRA☐   Other☐   Provide pertinent information:

1. _______________________________   _______________________________
        Type of Plan   Company Name / Contact

_______________________________   _______________________________
      Account Number   Phone

_______________________________   _______________________________
         Address   Name of Beneficiary

_______________________________   _______________________________
     Beneficiary Address   Beneficiary Phone Number

_______________________________   ____________/___________________
      Web site address   LOGIN INFO: User ID / Password

2. _______________________________   _______________________________
        Type of Plan   Company Name / Contact

_______________________________   _______________________________
      Account Number   Phone

_______________________________   _______________________________
         Address   Name of Beneficiary

_______________________________   _______________________________
     Beneficiary Address   Beneficiary Phone Number

_______________________________   ____________/___________________
      Web site address   LOGIN INFO: User ID / Password

3. _______________________________   _______________________________
        Type of Plan   Company Name / Contact

_______________________________   _______________________________
      Account Number   Phone

_______________________________   _______________________________
         Address   Name of Beneficiary

_______________________________   _______________________________
     Beneficiary Address   Beneficiary Phone Number

_______________________________   ____________/___________________
      Web site address   LOGIN INFO: User ID / Password

4. _______________________________   _______________________________
        Type of Plan   Company Name / Contact

A SENSE OF COMFORT
For You And Your Loved Ones

Account Number   Phone

Address   Name of Beneficiary

Beneficiary Address   Beneficiary Phone Number

Web site address   /   LOGIN INFO: User ID / Password

5. Type of Plan   Company Name / Contact

Account Number   Phone

Address   Name of Beneficiary

Beneficiary Address   Beneficiary Phone Number

Web site address   /   LOGIN INFO: User ID / Password

6. Type of Plan   Company Name / Contact

Account Number   Phone

Address   Name of Beneficiary

Beneficiary Address   Beneficiary Phone Number

Web site address   /   LOGIN INFO: User ID / Password

Do you collect Medicare, Medicaid, and/or Social Security benefits? ☐Yes ☐No

If yes, provide Medicare or Medicaid numbers and Social Security information:______________

____

* * * * *   * * * * *   * * * * *

ADDITIONAL INFORMATION FOR THIS SECTION:

* * * * * *   * * * * * *   * * * * * *

15. MILITARY SERVICE (Skip this section if you are not a military veteran)

Current status: ☐ACTIVE DUTY ☐RETIRED ☐RESERVE ☐ USAF ☐USA ☐USMC ☐USN

A copy of your DD Form 214 (Discharge papers) is located:_______________________

If retired, do you participate in the Survivor Benefit Plan (SBP)? ☐Yes ☐No

If retired, list any deductions currently being taken from your retirement pay:___________

____

If retired, list the name, relationship, address, and phone number of the beneficiary for any unpaid retiree pay at the time of your death:_______________________________________

____

Do you currently receive disability payments from Veterans Affairs? ☐Yes ☐No If yes, provide the following for any unpaid VA payments at the time of your death:

_________________________________   _______________________________
Beneficiary Name   Name

____
Relationship Address

Do you have any outstanding Veterans Affairs (VA) claims? ☐Yes ☐No If yes, where is the following located:
Copy of Claim____

VA Office being utilized:____

Contact Person:______________________________________ Phone:_______________

* * * * * *   * * * * * *   * * * * * *

ADDITIONAL INFORMATION FOR THIS SECTION:

____

____

____

____

____

____

ADDITIONAL INFORMATION FOR THIS SECTION:

* * * * * *   * * * * * *   * * * * * *

16. TAX INFORMATION

Where are copies located of your last 3 years of federal and state income tax filings?___________

____

If you use a tax preparer, list contact information:_________________________________

Name / Company

____   _____________________

Address   Phone

* * * * * *   * * * * * *   * * * * * *

17. OTHER ACCOUNT INFORMATION

Telephone Provider:____

  Account #_________________________________ Phone #_______________

TV Cable Provider:____

  Account #_________________________________ Phone #_______________

Internet Provider:____

  Account #_________________________________ Phone #_______________

Water/Sewage Provider:____

  Account #_________________________________ Phone #_______________

Natural Gas/Oil Provider:____

  Account #_________________________________ Phone #_______________

Electricity Provider:____

  Account #_________________________________ Phone #_______________

Trash Removal Company:____

  Account #_________________________________ Phone #_______________

Home Owners Association:____

  Account #_________________________________ Phone #_______________

Lawn / Yard Service:____

  Account #_________________________________ Phone #_______________

A SENSE OF COMFORT
For You And Your Loved Ones

Social Media:

    Facebook User ID: ______________________   Password: ______________________

    Twitter User ID: ______________________   Password: ______________________

    LinkedIn User ID: ______________________   Password: ______________________

Other:____

    Account #______________________________   Phone #________________

Other:____

    Account #______________________________   Phone #________________

* * * * * *   * * * * * *   * * * * * *

ADDITIONAL INFORMATION FOR THIS SECTION:

____

____

____

____

____

____

____

____

____

____

____

____

ADDITIONAL INFORMATION FOR THIS SECTION:

* * * * * *   * * * * * *   * * * * * *

18. SUBSCRIPTIONS / MEMBERSHIPS / PROFESSIONAL ORGANIZATIONS:

Newspaper: _________________________ Acct #_____________ Phone #_____________

Newspaper: _________________________ Acct #_____________ Phone #_____________

Newspaper: _________________________ Acct #_____________ Phone #_____________

Publication: _________________________ Acct #_____________ Phone #_____________

Magazine: _________________________ Acct #_____________ Phone #_____________

Magazine: _________________________ Acct #_____________ Phone #_____________

Magazine: _________________________ Acct #_____________ Phone #_____________

Professional Pub: _________________________ Acct #_____________ Phone #_____________

Professional Pub: _________________________ Acct #_____________ Phone #_____________

Automatic Renewals: _________________________ Acct #_____________ Phone #_____________

Automatic Deliveries: _________________________ Acct #_____________ Phone #_____________

Professional Dues: _________________________ Acct #_____________ Phone #_____________

Gym membership: _________________________ Acct #_____________ Phone #_____________

Charities: _________________________ Acct #_____________ Phone #_____________

Charities: _________________________ Acct #_____________ Phone #_____________

Other: __ _________________________ Acct #_____________ Phone #_____________

* * * * * *   * * * * * *   * * * * * *

ADDITIONAL INFORMATION FOR THIS SECTION:

____

____

____

____

A SENSE OF COMFORT
For You And Your Loved Ones

ADDITIONAL INFORMATION FOR THIS SECTION:

Now that you've completed Part I, please ensure that your loved one/personal representative is aware of: this workbook, its location, and that Parts II and III provide checklists and additional information to guide them.

Lastly, I want to reemphasize the need to safeguard this workbook, the personal information it contains, and to limit its access to only those with a need to know.

PART II

GOING INTO ACTION

* * * * * *   * * * * * *   * * * * * *

The death or incapacitation of a loved one creates many details to handle. The tasks can seem overwhelming, and worry or grief may make it difficult to take action or focus on priorities. The questions and answers identified in **Part I: Getting Prepared**, coupled with key information in this part will help you identify information you may need, and outline what steps you need to accomplish.

Make use of the extra space provided to take notes, capture important details, and record the date that the information was obtained.

* * * * * *   * * * * * *   * * * * * *

IF THE INDIVIDUAL IDENTIFIED IN PART I IS INCAPACITATED:

Refer to **Part I, Section 3, Health Care Directives** for details on the desires of the incapacitated person who needs medical care. Also, refer to the incapacitated person's estate plan documents, especially the Advanced Medical Directive and Living Will, if they exist.

If the incapacitated person has completed a Durable General Financial Power of Attorney (DGFPoA) that is acceptable to financial institutions, the person named as agent will be able to manage assets, sign a tax return, pay bills, or even sell property on behalf of the person incapacitated. See Part I, Section 2, Page 15/16 to determine if a DGFPoA was completed and who is named as agent.

☐Done ☐Not Applicable

Notes: ____

____

Many banks and brokerages are increasingly hesitant to accept the DGFPoA. If so, determine whether or not the person who is incapacitated signed the bank's, financial institution's, and/or brokerage house's power of attorney (PoA) form as a safeguard to ensure that the institution will allow the selected agent to act for him/her. See Part I, Section 2, Page 16 to determine if a PoA was completed and who is named as agent.

☐Done ☐Not Applicable

Notes: ____

____

If neither the DGFPoA nor the bank's, other financial institution's, or brokerage house's PoA forms were executed by the person incapacitated, it may be necessary to have a person serve as his/her guardian. See Part I, Section 2, Page 15/16 to determine if a guardian was named for the individual. Specific requirements and regulations are in place that should be met before filing to become a legal guardian. It is highly recommended that an estate attorney be consulted if filing for guardianship becomes necessary. This can differ from state to state, but the process usually goes through the following steps:

1. File a petition, usually in the jurisdiction where the person lives. You usually need to include medical documents or other sworn statements certifying that the person in question is incapable of making their own decisions.
2. An evaluation takes place.
3. If the person disputes the petition, a trial is held and the judge might ask for more evidence.
4. If the person does not dispute or is not capable to respond, a hearing takes place. Witnesses are called to support the need for a legal guardian. If the evidence supports

the need and you are considered an appropriate guardian, you are appointed as such by the judge.

☐Done ☐Not Applicable

Notes: ____

____

If the incapacitated person has a guardian, the guardian must be notified. See Part I, Sections 2 and 4, Page 16 to determine if a guardian has been appointed, and if so, how to contact the guardian.

☐Done ☐Not Applicable
Notes: ____

____

IF THE INDIVIDUAL IDENTIFIED IN PART I IS *DECEASED*:

Make the Right Call
For deaths that occur at home, it's important to know who to call. If your loved one is a hospice patient, call the hospice agency to report the death. A hospice provider will come to the home and pronounce the death. They may also call a mortuary for you and arrange for pick up of the body.

If your loved one is not a hospice patient, then you must call Emergency Services to notify the local police or sheriff of the death. A coroner or medical examiner may be required at the scene if the death was sudden.

☐Done ☐Not Applicable
Notes: ____

____

Contact the Funeral Home
Whether a hospice provider makes the call or you call yourself, a funeral home must be contacted to arrange for pick-up of the deceased. If funeral arrangements have already been made, you will only need to confirm the arrangements with the Funeral Director. Check the information in Part I, Section 10, Page 30 to determine whether or not a funeral/memorial was pre-arranged and/or pre-paid.

If no funeral arrangements have been made in advance, you will need to begin planning a funeral or memorial service. Check Part I, Section 10, Page 30 to determine whether or not the decedent wanted to be buried or cremated and whether or not he/she was an organ donor. You may want to call on relatives or close friends to assist in making the arrangements. See Part I, Section 10, Page 30 for a list of persons to be notified.

The funeral home can make arrangements to obtain certified copies of the death certificate. See **Part III, Other Information You Need to Know** for information on how many death certificates you will need.

☐Done ☐Not Applicable

A SENSE OF COMFORT
For You And Your Loved Ones

Notes: ____

____

Notifications

Contact relatives and those individuals identified by the deceased in Part I, Section 8, Pages 25, 26, and 30.

☐Done ☐Not Applicable

Notes: ____

____

Veterans Affairs

Check Part I, Section 15, Page 49 to determine if the deceased is entitled to Veterans Affairs (VA) benefits. If so, contact the VA at (800) 827-1000. The VA may offer help with funeral or burial costs as well as other benefits. For burial at Sea information, call (888) 647-6676 (option 4). Additionally, have any monthly payments stopped that the deceased may have been receiving.

☐Done ☐Not Applicable

Notes: ____

____

____

Notify the deceased's current employer (if applicable). See Part I, Section 1, Page 10.

☐Done ☐Not Applicable

Notes: ____

____

Contact any insurance companies as well as beneficiaries of the life insurance policies identified in Part I, Section 10, Page 36/37. Be prepared to provide policy numbers and a copy of the death certificate.

☐Done ☐Not Applicable

Notes: ____

____

If retired military, participating in the Survivor Benefit Program (SBP) or Retired Serviceman's Family Protection Plan (RSFPP), call one of the following numbers:

      Army, Air Force, Marine Corps, and Navy - (800) 321-1080
      US Coast Guard and NOAA - - - - - - - - - -(800) 772-8724
      US Public Health Service - - - - - - - - - - - -(800) 638-8744

☐Done ☐Not Applicable

Notes: ____

____

Contact the deceased's attorney, trust administrator, executor or representative of the estate. See Part I, Section 4, Page 19 and Section 8, Page 25 for information on each as applicable.

☐Done ☐Not Applicable
Notes: ____

____

If **you** are the deceased's trust administrator or executor, contact the court in the deceased's county to determine your responsibilities in this role.
☐Done ☐Not Applicable
Notes: ____

____

Contact the deceased's Attorney and arrange for the reading of the Will, if applicable.
☐Done ☐Not Applicable
Notes: ____

____

Contact the court and arrange for the probate process to be initiated, if required.
☐Done ☐Not Applicable
Notes: ____

____

Notify the Social Security Administration at (800) 772-1213 for Social Security survivor benefits, death benefits, and to stop Social Security payments to the deceased.

☐Done ☐Not Applicable
Notes: ____

____

If the deceased was entitled to retired military pay, contact the Defense Finance and Accounting Service (DFAS) at: (800) 321-1080 or (800) 269-5170.

☐Done ☐Not Applicable
Notes: ____

____

If the deceased was an annuitant of the Civil Service or Federal Employee Retirement System (CSRS or FERS), notify the office of Personnel Management (OPM) at (724) 794-2005.

☐Done ☐Not Applicable
Notes: ____

____

If the deceased participated in or was a CSRS or FERS retiree and participated in the Thrift Savings Plan (TSP) (See part I), contact the Federal retirement Thrift Investment Board at (877) 968-3778.

☐Done ☐Not Applicable
Notes: ____

____

If the deceased also qualified for a retirement plan or pension from a private sector employer, notify that employer or pension plan administrator. See part I, Section 1, page 10 if applicable.

☐Done ☐Not Applicable
Notes: ____

____

Notify any financial institution to include: banks, brokerages, mutual fund companies, transfer agents (for direct investment plans of individual stocks) and other investment firms that have individual or joint accounts in the name of the deceased. Make sure to have available account numbers and account statements. See Part I, Sections 13 and 14, pages 40-48 for details.

☐Done ☐Not Applicable
Notes: ____

____

See part I, Section 13-B on how to access investments and how they are being tracked/maintained.

☐Done ☐Not Applicable
Notes: ____

____

Notify credit card companies and other known creditors (e.g., telephone, water/sewage, gas, electric, trash removal, credit cards, mortgage/rental, home owners insurance, automobile insurance, shopping clubs, TV cable, etc.) Have account numbers available if known. See part I, Sections 11,12,13,17, and 18.

☐Done ☐Not Applicable
Notes: ____

____

Notify known debtors. Have details of money owed the deceased available. See Part I, Section 13-A, page 41.

☐Done ☐Not Applicable
Notes: ____

____

Contact accountant/CPA, financial advisor, and tax preparer, if known. See Part I, Section 13, Page 40. A determination needs to be made as to whether or not a final federal/state income tax return needs to be completed and whether or not a federal estate tax needs to be filed. If an estate tax return is required, make sure that it is completed and filed **within 9 months from the date of death**.

☐Done ☐Not Applicable

Notes: ____

____

Contact the postal service to forward mail to a new address, if applicable.

☐Done ☐Not Applicable

Notes: ____

____

Contact the deceased's other insurance companies (e.g., health, automobile, property). See Part I, Section 12, pages 36 – 39.

☐Done ☐Not Applicable

Notes: ____

____

Notify the deceased's mortgage company, if applicable. See part I, Section 11, Page 33.

☐Done ☐Not Applicable

Notes: ____

____

If deceased was renting, notify landlord. See Part I, Section 11, Page 33.

☐Done ☐Not Applicable

Notes: ____

____

Notify State Department of Motor Vehicles (DMV). Have the driver's license or number available. See Part I, Section 1, Page 10.

☐Done ☐Not Applicable

Notes: ____

____

If the deceased was leasing an automobile, contact the leasing company. See part I, Section 11, Page 34.

☐Done ☐Not Applicable

Notes: ____

____

Notify city, county, and state property offices.
☐Done ☐Not Applicable

Notes: ____

____

Cancel periodic subscriptions that deceased might have had. See Part I, Section 18, Page 54.
☐Done ☐Not Applicable

Notes: ____

____

Cancel other memberships or professional organizations with which the deceased had a relationship? See Part I, Section 18, Page 54.

☐Done ☐Not Applicable
Notes: ____

____

ADDITIONAL NOTES / INFORMATION:

____

____

____

____

____

____

____

____

____

____

____

____

ADDITIONAL NOTES / INFORMATION:

PART III

OTHER THINGS
YOU NEED TO KNOW

Information in this part may change periodically. For the most current information, visit the Nelson Financial Planning Services, LLC website at: www.fnfps.com.

DEATH CERTIFICATES

How Many Copies of Death Certificates Will You need?

Certified copies of the death certificate are not required to claim social security lump sum benefits or to apply for survivor benefits. Only a "verification of death" is required.

Certified copies of the Death Certificate may be required for the following transactions. Funeral homes can make arrangements to supply them to you.

- The transfer of an individual CHECKING ACCOUNT or a "Joint" checking account if it is in the name of more than one person without "or" or "and/or" appearing in the account's ownership.

- Transfer of an individual SAVINGS ACCOUNT OF A "Joint" savings account if it is not an "and/or" account.

- Transfer of an individual SAFE DEPOSIT BOX or a safe deposit box in the name of other parties unless the ownership is taken as "or".

- Transfer of each TITLE OF REAL ESTATE OWNERSHIP. This applies to property with the title taken as "Joint Tenancy with the Right of Survivorship."

- Transfer of each TITLE OF OWNERSHIP FOR all registered motor vehicles. (Multiple manes on the title does not apply if the work "or" "and/or" appears on the title between the manes of the registered owners.)

- One for each LIFE INSURANCE POLICY claim. (If there are multiple policies with one single company, a separate certified copy of the death certificate may be required for each policy number.)

- One for each claim for BURIAL or FUNERAL INSURANCE plan.

- One for each death benefit claim from a UNIION.

- Transfer of ownership of STOCK. One for each transaction of the stock is sold or transferred separately.

- Transfer or redemption of BONDS.

- Transfer or redemption of TREASURY BILLS (T-Bills).

- Transfer or redemption of CERTIFICATES OF DEPOSIT (CD'S).

- Transfer or redemption of MONEY MARKET ACCOUNTS.

- To "roll-over" an IRA account.

- Federal and State Tax Returns

A SENSE OF COMFORT
For You And Your Loved Ones

ESTATE PLANNING ATTORNEY

How To Find An Estate Planning Attorney

Use the following largest online estate planning lawyers' directory to quickly find detailed profiles of attorneys and law firms in your area.

http://lawyers.findlaw.com/lawyer/practice/Estate-Planning

Questions to Ask Before Hiring an Estate Planning Attorney

Before hiring an estate planning attorney to help you develop an estate plan, ask any potential candidate the following questions. This will ensure that you don't end up paying a whole lot of money for services that are not what you need, expect or want. Hiring an attorney does not have to be a fearful experience. It can be one of the most empowered decision you ever make for yourself.

1. What is your education and experience? Does your practice focus on estate planning?

2. What will happen during an initial meeting with your office and how much will it cost?

3. Are all of your fees flat fees? What is included in the flat fee? What is NOT included in the flat fee? What happens when I call with legal questions after my planning documents were completed? What if the questions are about something other than my estate plan?

4. What happens when things change in my life? Do you notify me about changes in the law?

5. Does my planning fee include a regular review of my plan? What if I want to make changes to my plan?

6. Do you have a process for helping me capture and pass on my intangible wealth, such as my intellectual, spiritual and human assets or who I am and what's important to me or do you primarily focus on financial assets?

7. Do you have an estate planning maintenance program or membership program for ongoing service and, if so, what does it include?

8. Can you assist me with both simple and advanced estate planning? Can you help me evaluate tools to minimize my estate taxation and protect the wealth for which I have worked so hard?

9. Do you make sure my assets are titled in the right way? How?

10. Can you structure my estate plan so that whatever I leave to my kids will be protected from a lawsuit against them or if they are divorced in the future? How often do you build that kind of planning into clients' plans?

11. Do you prepare a comprehensive plan for my kids' care if something happens to me, like the Kids Protection Plan™ that names short and long-term guardians and gives specific instructions to all of the guardians and my caregivers? What about an ID card for my wallet listing the short-term guardians with their contact information?

12. Do you have a whole team in place or is it just you? What happens if something happens to you or you retire?

13. What happens if I need to get a quick question answered and you are not available?

Knowing the answer to these questions before you hire an estate planning attorney will ensure that you put in place an estate plan for your family that will work when your family needs it most.

FINANCIAL PLANNER

How to Choose a Financial Advisor from www.cfp.net

You may be considering help from a financial planner for a number of reasons, whether it's deciding to buy a new home, planning for retirement or your children's education, or simply not having the time or expertise to get your finances in order. Whatever your needs, working with a financial planner can be a helpful step in securing your financial future.

You should interview and evaluate several financial planners to find the one that's right for you. You will want to select a competent, qualified professional with whom you feel comfortable, one whose business style suits your financial planning needs.

10 Questions to Ask When Choosing a Financial Planner

1 **Q. What experience do you have?**

A. Find out how long the planner has been in practice and the number and types of companies with which she has been associated. Ask the planner to briefly describe his/her work experience and how it relates to his/her current practice. Choose a financial planner who has experience counseling individuals on their financial needs.

2 **Q. What are your qualifications?**

A. The term "financial planner" is used by many financial professionals. Ask the planner what qualifies him/her to offer financial planning advice and whether he is recognized as a CERTIFIED FINANCIAL PLANNER™ professional or CFP® practitioner, a Certified Public Accountant-Personal Financial Specialist (CPA-PFS), or a Chartered Financial Consultant (ChFC). Look for a planner who has proven experience in financial planning topics such as insurance, tax planning, investments, estate planning or retirement planning. Determine what steps the planner takes to stay current with changes and developments in the financial planning field. If the planner holds a financial planning designation or certification, check on his background with CFP Board or other relevant professional organizations.

3 **Q. What services do you offer?**

A. The services a financial planner offers depend on a number of factors including credentials, licenses and areas of expertise. Generally, financial planners cannot sell insurance or securities products such as mutual funds or stocks without the proper licenses, or give investment advice unless registered with state or Federal authorities. Some planners offer financial planning advice on a range of topics but do not sell financial products. Others may provide advice only in specific areas such as estate planning or on tax matters.

4 **Q. What is your approach to financial planning?**

A. Ask the financial planner about the type of clients and financial situations she typically likes to work with. Some planners prefer to develop one plan by bringing together all of your financial goals. Others provide advice on specific areas, as needed.

Make sure the planner's viewpoint on investing is not too cautious or overly aggressive for you. Some planners require you to have a certain net worth before offering services. Find out if the planner will carry out the financial recommendations developed for you or refer you to others who will do so.

5 **Q. Will you be the only person working with me?**

A. The financial planner may work with you himself or have others in the office assist him/her. You may want to meet everyone who will be working with you. If the planner works with professionals outside his/her own practice (such as attorneys, insurance agents or tax specialists) to develop or carry out financial planning recommendations, get a list of their names to check on their backgrounds.

6 **Q. How will I pay for your services?**

A. As part of your financial planning agreement, the financial planner should clearly tell you in writing how he/she will be paid for the services to be provided. Planners can be paid in several ways: A salary paid by the company for which the planner works. The planner's employer receives payment from you or others, either in fees or commissions, in order to pay the planner's salary. Fees based on an hourly rate, a flat rate, or on a percentage of your assets and/or income. Commissions paid by a third party from the products sold to you to carry out the financial planning recommendations. Commissions are usually a percentage of the amount you invest in a product. A combination of fees and commissions whereby fees are charged for the amount of work done to develop financial planning recommendations and commissions are received from any products sold. In addition, some planners may offset some portion of the fees you pay if they receive commissions for carrying out their recommendations.

7 **Q. How much do you typically charge?**

A. While the amount you pay the planner will depend on your particular needs, the financial planner should be able to provide you with an estimate of possible costs based on the work to be performed. Such costs should include the planner's hourly rates or flat fees or the percentage he would receive as commission on products you may purchase as part of the financial planning recommendations.

8 **Q. Could anyone besides me benefit from your recommendations?**

A. Some business relationships or partnerships that a planner has could affect his/her professional judgment while working with you, inhibiting the planner from acting in your best interest. Ask the planner to provide you with a description of his/her conflicts of interest in writing. For example, financial planners who sell insurance policies, securities or mutual funds have a business relationship with the companies that provide these financial products. The planner may also have relationships or partnerships that should be disclosed to you, such as business he/she receives for referring you to an insurance agent, accountant or attorney for implementation of planning suggestions.

9 **Q. Have you ever been publicly disciplined for any unlawful or unethical actions in your professional career?**

A. Several government and professional regulatory organizations, such as FINRA (formerly NASD), your state insurance and securities departments, and CFP Board keep records on the disciplinary history of financial planners and advisers. Ask what organizations the planner is regulated by and contact these groups to conduct a background check. All financial planners who have registered as investment advisers with the Securities and Exchange Commission or state securities agencies, or who are associated with a company that is registered as an investment adviser, must be able to provide you with a disclosure form called Form ADV Part II or the state equivalent of that form.

10 **Q. Can I have it in writing?**

A. Ask the planner to provide you with a written agreement that details the services that will be provided. Keep this document in your files for future reference.

FUNERAL PLANNING

The Funeral Consumers Alliance (FCA) is a nonprofit organization dedicated to protecting consumer's right to choose a meaningful, dignified, and affordable funeral. If you prefer simply arrangements, you will find their information on services, caskets, embalming, and cremation helpful. They are located at 33 Patchen Road, South Burlington, VT 05403. Phone (800) 765-0107. To learn more visit www.funerals.org.

The Federal Trade Commission's (FTC) Consumer Response Center offers a free copy of "Funerals: A Consumer Guide" and additional information concerning the Funeral Rule on its website. The FTC is located at 600 Pennsylvania Ave, NW, Room H-130, Washington, DC 20580-0001. Phone (877) 382-4357. Visit www.ftc.gov/funerals/ to learn more.

HOSPICE / PALLIATIVE CARE

Care Connections, is a program of the National Hospice and Palliative Care organization. It provides people with information and support when they are planning ahead, caring for a loved one, living with illness or grieving a loss. They provide state-specific forms on advance directives. They are located at 1700 Diagonal Road, Suite #615, Alexandria, VA 22314. Phone (800) 658-8898. Visit www.caringinfo.org to learn more.

INVESTMENTS

Why certain classes of investments should be sold before others?

The key thing to know about sequencing those withdrawals is that you want to get rid of things that are costing you the most tax-wise first. So, if you are over 70 and a half and taking required minimum distributions (RMD) from your retirement accounts, you obviously want to take those, because you'll pay big penalties if you do not.

Investments in taxable accounts that generate interest such as savings, checking, money market, bond mutual funds, and CDs and investments that generate short-term capital gains are taxed at ordinary income tax rates. These types of investments should be considered for selling next because there are no tax breaks for them.

Investments that provide for favorable tax treatments should be sold after the ones which do not. Investments in taxable accounts that are held for more than 365 days are considered long-term investments. Once sold, if there is a gain, the gain is taxed at the more favorable long-term tax rate (currently 15% maximum). If sold at a loss, the loss is considered a long-term capital loss and long-term capital losses offset long-term capital gains. The same is true for short-term gains and losses. Additionally, once long-terms gains and losses are computed and then short-term gains and losses are computed, they are added together. Net losses offset any net gains.

Although IRAs, 401k plans and other retirement plans do not have short or long-term gains and losses, they receive favorable tax consideration because the accounts can grow tax deferred for several years. Once distributions are taken, they are taxed at ordinary income tax rates. In the case of Roth IRAs held for five years or more, when distributions are taken, the gains are never taxed. **So, investments held in Roth accounts should be the very last to be sold.** With the exception of RMD, investments in retirement accounts should be sold after investments in taxable accounts. RMD of traditional IRAs, 401k, 403b plans, and other retirement accounts must begin by age 70 ½. RMD is based on the life expectancy of the person receiving distributions as well as the account balances at the end of the previous year. The IRS publishes tables which show life expectancies based on current ages of the tax payers. For example, if a person is 71 years old, their life expectancy might be 15 years. So, if they would be required to make annual distributions from their retirements accounts over the next 15 years. The amount to be distributed is based on the balance of their retirement accounts on December 31 of each year. There is no RMD for Roth IRAs, so Roth IRAs can grow indefinitely.

When investments in taxable accounts are sold, what needs to be reported to the IRS?

The IRS requires the following information on the tax return: *name of investment, number of shares purchased, date purchased, amount paid (cost basis), number of shares sold, date sold, and amount received.* If a person cannot show the IRS what was paid for the investment, the IRS assumes that the cost basis is zero and the person will pay taxes on the entire amount received. A major mistake that many investors make is not including reinvested dividends and capital gains in cost basis. Not doing so will result in paying higher taxes than is required.

What is the tax treatment of investments sold in retirement accounts?

For 401k, 403b, 457, SEP IRAs, Traditional IRA and other retirement accounts where the contributions were tax deductible, when investments are sold, the distributions are taxed at your ordinary income tax rate. For traditional IRAs where the contributions were not tax deductible, since the contributions were already taxed, only the gains will be taxed when the investments are sold. In the case of Roth IRAs and Roth 401k plans, as long as the Roth was in existence for at least 5 years, there won't be any taxes on the distribution. In the above cases, it's assumed that the individual sold the investments after the minimum age of $59^{1/2}$ and no penalties existed.

LEGAL ASSISTANCE (for Elders / People with Special Needs)

National Academy of Elder Law Attorneys (NAELA) is a professional association of attorneys who are dedicated to improving the quality of legal services provided to seniors and people with special needs. NAELA examines and advocates on public policy issues facing seniors and people with special needs, but does not provide direct legal services. Although NAELA does not provide direct legal services, it has a membership of more than 4200 professionals. NAELA is located at 1877 Spring Hill Road, Ste 220, Vienna, VA 22182. Phone (703) 942-5711. Go to www.naela.org for more information.

A SENSE OF COMFORT
For You And Your Loved Ones

The National Elder Law Foundation (NELF) operates an elder law certification program for attorneys. Applicants must pass a full day certification examination and prove that they have current experience in elder law among other criteria. Successful applicants receive the Certified Elder Law Attorney designation. NELF is located at 6336 N. oracle Road, Ste. 326, #136, Tucson, AZ 84704. Phone (520) 881-1076. Go to www.nelf.org for more information.

LIFE INSURANCE

TERM INSURANCE provides a preset amount of cash if you die while the policy is in force. For example, a ten-year $130,000 term policy pays off if you die within ten years -- and that's it. If you live beyond the end of the term, you get nothing. With term insurance, you pay only for life insurance coverage. The policy does not develop reserves. If you need insurance for only a short time, (e.g., to qualify for a business loan), term is your best option.

Term insurance is the cheapest form of coverage over a limited number of years, especially when you're younger. It is particularly suitable for younger parents who want substantial insurance coverage at lower cost. Since the risk of dying in your 20s, 30s or 40s is quite low, the cost of term insurance during these years is as reasonable as life insurance prices get. However, the older you are, the more expensive term insurance premiums become compared to the payoff value of the policy. This, of course, is understandable, as the older you are, the greater the chance you will die during the policy term.

Term policies offered by different companies have all sorts of differences, some fairly significant. For example, some policies are automatically renewable at the end of the term without a medical examination, often for higher premiums, and some are not. Some have premiums set for a period of years, but others guarantee a premium rate for only the first year. After that, the rate can go up. Some can also be converted from a term to 'whole life' or 'universal' policy during the term, again without needing to re-qualify. But remember, with term insurance you never lock in the right to maintain the policy no matter how old you become. If you want to ensure that insurance will continue in force for your entire life, term isn't for you

PERMANENT INSURANCE is much more expensive than term insurance. Why buy it? It can never be canceled as long as you pay the premiums, and because it's also an investment.

With a permanent policy, your premium payments for the first few (or more than a few) years cover more than the insurance company's cost of your risk of death. The excess money goes into a reserve account, which is invested by the insurance company. Unless the company is disastrously managed, these investments yield returns in the form of interest or dividends. A proportion of these are passed along to you. You can add these returns to your policy reserves or borrow against them, after a set time. And if you decide to end the policy, you can cash it in for the "surrender value." Returns that accumulate are not taxable, unless the money is actually distributed to you. Certain partial withdrawals can even be made without paying tax. By contrast, the interest on bank accounts is subject to tax in the year it is paid, even if left untouched in the account.

However, although permanent insurance policies do function as an investment, maximizing your investment return is not the purpose of insurance. If that's what you want, you'd probably do better buying cheaper term insurance and putting the money you save in other tax-deferred investments. There are a number of types of permanent life insurance. The following describes them.

74

WHOLE LIFE INSURANCE (sometimes called "Straight Life") provides a set dollar amount of coverage that can never be canceled in exchange for fixed, uniform payments. Because the payments are the same throughout your life, the premiums are higher compared to your statistical risk of death in the early years of the policy. This is why reserves are built up. Assuming you live a long time after the policy was issued, your payments become lower -- compared to your risk of death. In other words, during the first few years of a whole life policy, insurance companies take in substantially more money than they pay out.

Some of the surplus goes to pay the insurance agent's commission. Some of it becomes your cash reserve, which the company puts in fixed-income investments. After a set time, usually several years, you have the right to borrow against the cash reserve. You can also, of course, cancel the policy and receive its cash surrender value.

Whole life is generally undesirable for younger people with small children who can't afford the high premiums during the early years of the policy.

UNIVERSAL LIFE INSURANCE combines some of the desirable features of both term and whole life insurance, and offers other advantages, including:
- Over time, the net cost is lower than whole life insurance.
- You build up a cash reserve, as with whole life.
- You can vary the premium payments, amount of coverage, or both, from year to year. In contrast, whole life requires one set payment amount, which cannot be varied, for the life of the policy. In addition, universal life policies normally provide you with more consumer information. For example, you are told how much of your premium goes toward company overhead expenses, reserves and policy proceed payments, and how much is retained for your savings. This information isn't usually provided with whole life policies.

VARIABLE LIFE INSURANCE refers to policies in which cash reserves are invested in securities, stocks, and bonds. In a sense, these policies combine an insurance feature with a mutual fund. That means your investment return is tied to the financial markets' performance.

VARIABLE UNIVERSAL LIFE INSURANCE is a type of whole life insurance that combines the premium payment and coverage flexibility of universal life insurance with the investment opportunity (and risk) of variable life insurance.

SINGLE-PREMIUM LIFE INSURANCE is one in which you pay, up-front, all premiums due for the full duration of the policy. Normally, any policy with a savings feature can be purchased with a single premium. Obviously, this requires a large chunk of cash -- $5,000, $10,000 or often much more, depending on your age and the dollar amount of the policy.

One reason to commit so much cash to buying an insurance policy is that it enables you to give the fully-paid-for policy to new owners, which can result in major estate tax savings. Because there are no more payments to make, a gift of a single-premium policy doesn't involve the risk that the new owners will fail to make payments and cause the policy to be canceled.

SURVIVORSHIP LIFE INSURANCE (also called "second to die," or "joint," insurance) provides a single policy that insures two lives, usually spouses. When the first spouse dies, no proceeds are paid. Instead, the policy remains in force and the surviving spouse must continue to pay premiums. The policy pays off only upon the death of the second spouse.

Why would any couple want such a policy? Wealthier couples who expect that substantial estate taxes will be assessed on the death of the second spouse may use survivorship life insurance as part of estate planning.

This type of insurance may also be desirable when a major family asset is a valuable family business, or real estate interests -- assets that aren't liquid, and that the survivors may not want to sell. Or suppose two children inherit a family business, but one doesn't want to keep it going. The other could use her share of the insurance proceeds as an initial buy-out payment, so he/she could retain ownership of the business.

Finally, this kind of insurance may be desirable if one member of a couple is in less than good health, making other types of insurance extremely expensive. Because two lives are insured, premiums for survivorship life policies are relatively low compared to policies on one person's life. Therefore, if the other spouse is in reasonably good health, the couple can usually obtain survivorship life insurance.

How are proceeds from life insurance treated from a tax standpoint?

Beneficiaries are not taxed on the proceeds they receive from life insurance. However, if the deceased owned the insurance policy, then the proceeds are included in his/her gross estate and might be subject to estate taxes (state and/or federal). The proceeds of the life insurance policy pass to the beneficiaries by process of law and are **not** subject to probate.

What options are there for life insurance proceeds?

Settlement options determine how the proceeds of the policy will be distributed upon the death of the insured. The usual choices available to the beneficiaries are: (1) to have the proceeds paid in a lump sum, (2) to have the proceeds distributed as a periodic income of some fixed amount for as long as the capital sum and investment income permit, (3) to have the proceeds distributed over a fixed number of months or years, and (4) to have the proceeds paid as a life income to the beneficiary, perhaps with a minimum period certain or refund feature.

MILITARY DISCHARGE PAPERS (DD Form 214)

If you cannot find the original, you may request a copy by calling 800-318-5298, or by going to the National Archives website (www.archives.gov) and following the link for veterans and their families.

MILITARY SERVICES CONTACT INFORMATION

Defense Finance and Accounting Service
U S Military Retirement Pay
Post Office Box 7130
London, KY 40742 7130
(800) 321-1080 or (216) 522-5955/(800) 269-5170 (for deceased members)

A SENSE OF COMFORT
For You And Your Loved Ones

Department of Navy
NPC   PERS-675R
Retired Activities Section
5720 Integrity Drive
Millington, TN 38055-6640
(866) 827-5672

U.S. Army
Office of the Deputy Chief of Staff, G-1
DAPE-HRPD-RSO (Retirement Services Office)
200 Stovall St.
Alexandria, VA 22332-0470
(703) 325-9158

U.S. Air Force
AFPC/DPPRT
550 C Street W, Ste 3
Randolph AFB, TX 78150-4713
(210) 565-4663

U.S. Marine Corps
Headquarters, USMC
Manpower and Reserve Affairs
(MMSR-6)
3280 Russell Road
Quantico, VA 22134-5103
(800) 336-4649 Option #0

U.S. Coast Guard
Commanding Officer (RAS)
U. S. Coast Guard
Personnel Service Center
444 SE Quincy St
Topeka KS 66683-3591
(800) 772-8724

PROBATE

Probate is the legal process of locating and assessing a deceased person's assets, paying the deceased's financial obligations and then distributing whatever is left over to the deceased's heirs. As a result, probate can be   a long and expensive process, taking months and sometimes years, while chipping away at the value of the estate. Accordingly, most people strive to avoid probate. For information on how to avoid probate, go to the   following website:

http://estate.findlaw.com/probate/how-to-avoid-probate.html/?DCMP=GOO-EST_Probate Avoid&HBX_PK=how+to+avoid+probate

For information on when probate is necessary and the steps of the probate process, refer to the following websites.

http://www.estatesettlement.com/ftf_stepsprocess.php

http://www.probateprocess.org/

http://www.nolo.com/legal-encyclopedia/how-probate-process-works-information-32438.html

http://www.dummies.com/how-to/content/probing-probate-what-you-should-know.html

http://wills.about.com/od/howtoavoidprobate/tp/necessaryprobate.htm

PROBATE INITIATION

An "executor" or "personal representative" is a person designated in the Will by the deceased person (decedent) to distribute the decedent's estate to heirs and beneficiaries. It is the executor of the estate who generally initiates the probate legal process. Probate involves a number of legal proceedings in the state probate court to determine whether the Will is valid and to oversee distribution:

- First, the executor must locate the Will and death certificate.
- Then he/she notifies all employers, government agencies, and financial organizations of the death.
- Next, the executor usually contacts an attorney to help him/her deal with the probate court and determine whether probate is even necessary.

If the estate is valued over a certain amount, the attorney, in the name of the executor, will file the correct forms with the probate court. Some states require that the executor hire an attorney. Documents filed include the Will, a "petition for administration," "notice of appointment and pendency of probate," etc., along with applicable court fees.

While it is the executor's duty to initiate probate, any person with an interest in the estate can initiate probate if the executor has failed to do so. For example, with debtor estates, beneficiaries may have little incentive to start probate, and so the creditors will have to step in to start the process in order to get what little assets remain. In addition, possible beneficiaries may start probate if a named executor delays in filing (e.g., is suspected of stealing assets in the estate). If a possible beneficiary does not have the Will in hand, she may file for probate under the state laws of "intestacy," meaning how the estate is to be distributed if there is no Will. The probate court will consider the circumstances and may appoint any other person as executor if the executor named in the Will has not fulfilled her duties.

REGISTER OF WILLS

The Office of Register of Wills is a public office established under the Constitution of the State. The Constitution provides for a Register from each county and/or city. Each Register is elected by qualified voters.

The Register of Wills is responsible for appointing personal representatives to administer decedents' estates and for overseeing the proper and timely administration of these proceedings. They also perform the following duties: assist and advise the public in the preparation of all required forms; maintain and preserve the permanent record of all proceedings; serve as the Clerk to the Orphans' Court; track estates and refer delinquent matters to the Court; determine and collect inheritance taxes and probate fees/court costs; audit accounts of personal representatives and guardians; mail various notices and court orders to interested persons; and, verify compliance with court orders. As a service we provide safekeeping for wills of living persons.

RETIREMENT ACCOUNTS

Retirement accounts (401k, 403b, 457 Plans, Traditional and Roth IRAs, etc.) pass by process of law to beneficiaries and are **not subjected to the probate process**. Unlike taxable accounts, retirement accounts do not receive a step-up in basis. Only a spouse of a deceased person can roll over the assets in retirement accounts into their own retirement accounts. As such they can extend the tax deferment (or in the case of Roth IRAs tax exemption) until age 701/2 before required minimum distributions must be made.

Other beneficiaries of retirement accounts cannot transfer deceased's retirement accounts into their own. Beneficiaries can roll over the accounts into Inherited IRAs and can therefore extend the accounts throughout their lifetimes. The beneficiaries must make required minimum distributions from these accounts each year based on their life expectancy.

Inheriting an IRA or other retirement accounts

Properly dealing with an inherited IRA can be tricky. If you take the right steps, you can continue to delay taxation on the account for many years. However, if you make a mistake, the entire account balance could be taxable immediately — thereby wasting a potentially huge sum of money on taxes. When you inherit an IRA, the rules that apply to you depend on whether or not the deceased account owner was your spouse.

Inherited IRA: Spouse Beneficiary

As a spouse beneficiary, you have two primary options:

- Do a spousal rollover — rolling the account into your own IRA, or
- Continue to own the account as a beneficiary.

Note: There's no deadline on a spousal rollover. You can own the account as a beneficiary for several years, then elect to do a spousal rollover. If you do a spousal rollover, from that point forward, it will be as if the IRA was yours to begin with. All the normal IRA rules will apply — whether Roth or traditional. If you continue to own the account as a beneficiary, the rules will be mostly the same, with a few important exceptions:

- **No 10% Penalty** - First, you can take distributions from the account without being subject to the 10% penalty, regardless of your age. So if you expect to need the money prior to age $59^{1/2}$, this is a good reason not to go the spousal rollover route — at least not yet. (As mentioned above, there's no deadline on a spousal rollover.)

- **Withdrawals from Inherited Roth IRA** - Second, if the inherited account was a Roth IRA, any withdrawals of earnings taken prior to the point at which the original owner would have satisfied the 5-year rule will be subject to income tax (though not the 10% penalty).

- **Spouse Beneficiary RMDs** - Third, if the inherited account was a traditional IRA, you'll have to start taking Required Minimum Distributions (RMD) in the year in which the deceased account owner would have been required to take them, rather than the year in which you would ordinarily be required to take them. At that point, however, the distributions will be calculated the same as if it were your own account. (That is, each year, the RMD will be based on your own remaining life expectancy.)

Note: If the original owner (your spouse) was required to take an RMD in the year in which he/she died, but he/she had not yet taken it, you're required to take it for him/her — calculated in the same way it would be if he/she were still alive.

Inherited IRA: Non-Spouse Beneficiary

When you inherit an IRA as a non-spouse beneficiary, the account works much like a typical IRA, with three important exceptions.

- **No 10% Penalty** - Distributions from the account are not subject to the 10% penalty, regardless of your age. (This is the same as for a spouse beneficiary.)

- **Withdrawals from Inherited Roth IRA** - If the inherited account was a Roth IRA, any withdrawals of earnings taken prior to the point at which the original owner would have satisfied the 5-year rule will be subject to income tax, though not the 10% penalty. (This is also the same as for a spouse beneficiary.)

- **Non-Spouse Beneficiary RMDs** - Each year, beginning in the year after the death of the account owner, you'll have to take a Required Minimum Distribution (RMD) from the account. The idea is to distribute the balance of the account over your remaining life expectancy. The actual calculations are best explained with an example.

Imagine that your grandfather passes away in 2011, leaving you his entire IRA. If he was required to take an RMD in 2011 but he had not yet taken one, you'll be required to take his RMD for him — calculated in the same way it would be if he were still alive.

RMDs from the account are based on your life expectancy. For example, if on your birthday in 2012, you turn 31 years old, according to the IRS Life Expectancy Tables, your remaining life expectancy at age 30 is 53.3 years. As a result, your RMD for 2012 will be equal to the account balance as of 12/31/2011, divided by 53.3.

For 2012, your RMD will be equal to the account balance at the end of 2011, divided by 52.3. In 2013, it'll be the end of 2012 balance, divided by 51.3.

Important exception: If you want, you can elect to distribute the account over 5 years rather than over your remaining life expectancy. If you elect to do that, you can take the distributions however you'd like over those five years — for example, no distributions in years 1-3 and everything in year 4.

Successor Beneficiary RMDs

If the original non-spouse beneficiary dies before the account has been fully distributed, the *new* inheriting beneficiary is known as a successor beneficiary. Successor beneficiaries are subject to the same rules as the original beneficiary, with one exception: The successor beneficiary must continue to take distributions each year as if they were the original beneficiary.

By way of illustration, in the example above, if you had died in 2013, leaving the entire IRA to your sister, she would be required to continue taking RMDs from the account according to the exact same schedule you had been taking them, regardless of her own age. So if you hadn't yet taken your 2013 distribution, she'd have to take it. Her 2014 distribution would be exactly what yours would have been if you were still alive: the 12/31/2013 balance, divided by 50.3.

Tips for Non-Spouse Beneficiaries

- When you re-title the account, be sure to include both your name *and* the name of the original owner.

- Name new beneficiaries for the account ASAP.

- If you decide to move the account to another custodian (to Vanguard from Edward Jones, for instance), do a direct transfer only. If you attempt to execute a regular rollover and you end up in possession of the funds, it will count as if you'd distributed the entire account.

Inherited IRA: Multiple Beneficiaries

If multiple beneficiaries inherit an IRA, they're each treated as if they were non-spouse beneficiaries, and they each have to use the life expectancy of the oldest beneficiary when calculating RMDs. This is not a good thing, as it means less ability to "stretch" the IRA.

However, if the beneficiaries split the IRA into separate inherited IRAs by the end of the year following the year of the original owner's death, then each beneficiary gets to treat his own inherited portion as if he were the sole beneficiary of an IRA of that size. This is a good thing, because it means that:

- A spouse beneficiary will be treated as a spouse beneficiary rather than as a non-spouse beneficiary (thereby allowing for more distribution options), and

- Each non-spouse beneficiary will get to use his or her own life expectancy for calculating RMDs.

To split an inherited IRA into separate inherited IRAs:

- Create a separate account for each beneficiary, titled to include both the name of the deceased owner as well as the beneficiary.

- Use direct, trustee-to-trustee transfers to move the assets from the original IRA to each of the separate inherited IRA accounts.

- Change the Social Security Number on each account to be that of the applicable beneficiary.

REVERSE MORTGAGE

Top 10 Things to Know if You're Interested in a Reverse Mortgage.

A SENSE OF COMFORT
For You And Your Loved Ones

The Home Equity Conversion Mortgage (HECM) is FHA's reverse mortgage program, which enables you to withdraw some of the equity in your home. The HECM is a safe plan that can give older Americans greater financial security. Many seniors use it to supplement Social Security, meet unexpected medical expenses, and make home improvements and more. You can receive additional free information about reverse mortgages in general by contacting the National Council on Aging at (800) 510-0301 or downloading their free booklet, **"Use Your Home to Stay at Home,"** a guide for older homeowners who need help now. It is smart to know more about reverse mortgages, and decide if one is right for you!

1. What is a reverse mortgage?

A reverse mortgage is a special type of home loan that lets you convert a portion of the equity in your home into cash. The equity that you built up over years of making mortgage payments can be paid to you. However, unlike a traditional home equity loan or second mortgage, HECM borrowers do not have to repay the HECM loan until the borrowers no longer use the home as their principal residence or fail to meet the obligations of the mortgage. You can also use a HECM to purchase a primary residence if you are able to use cash on hand to pay the difference between the HECM proceeds and the sales price plus closing costs for the property you are purchasing.

2. Can I qualify for FHA's HECM reverse mortgage?

To be eligible for a FHA HECM, the FHA requires that you be a homeowner 62 years of age or older, own your home outright, or have a low mortgage balance that can be paid off at closing with proceeds from the reverse loan, and you **must** live in the home. You are also required to receive consumer information free or at very low cost from a HECM counselor prior to obtaining the loan. You can find a **HECM counselor online** or by phoning (800) 569-4287.

3. Can I apply for a HECM even if I did not buy my present house with FHA mortgage insurance?

Yes. You may apply for a HECM regardless of whether or not you purchased your home with an FHA-insured mortgage.

4. What types of homes are eligible?

To be eligible for the FHA HECM, your home must be a single family home or a 2-4 unit home with one unit occupied by the borrower. HUD-approved condominiums and manufactured homes that meet FHA requirements are also eligible.

5. What are the differences between a reverse mortgage and a home equity loan?

With a second mortgage, or a home equity line of credit, borrowers must have adequate income to qualify for the loan, and they make monthly payments on the principal and interest. A reverse mortgage is different, because it pays you – there are no monthly principal and interest payments. With a reverse mortgage, you are required to pay real estate taxes, utilities, and hazard and flood insurance premiums.

6. Will we have an estate that we can leave to heirs?

When the home is sold or no longer used as a primary residence, the cash, interest, and other HECM finance charges must be repaid. All proceeds beyond the amount owed belong to your spouse or estate. This means any remaining equity can be transferred to heirs. No debt is passed along to the estate or heirs.

7. How much money can I get from my home?

The amount you may borrower will depend on:

- Age of the youngest borrower
- Current interest rate
- Lesser of appraised value or the HECM FHA mortgage limit of $625,500 or the sales price; and
- Initial Mortgage Insurance Premium--your choices are HECM Standard or HECM SAVER

You can borrow more with the HECM Standard option. In addition, the more valuable your home is, the older you are, and the lower the interest rate, the more you can borrow. If there is more than one borrower, the age of the youngest borrower is used to determine the amount you can borrow. For an estimate of HECM cash benefits, select the online calculator from the **HECM Home Page**. Many online reverse mortgage calculators can provide you with an estimate of the amount of funds you can borrow.

8. Should I use an estate planning service to find a reverse mortgage lender?

FHA does NOT recommend using any service that charges a fee for referring a borrower to an FHA-approved lender. You can locate a FHA-approved lender by searching online at **www.hud.gov** or by contacting a HECM counselor for a listing. Services rendered by HECM counselors are free or at a low cost. To locate a HECM counselor **Search online** or call (800) 569-4287 toll-free, for the name and location of a HUD-approved housing counseling agency near you.

9. How do I receive my payments?

You can select from five payment plans:

- **Tenure**- equal monthly payments as long as at least one borrower lives and continues to occupy the property as a principal residence.
- **Term**- equal monthly payments for a fixed period of months selected.
- **Line of Credit**- unscheduled payments or in installments, at times and in an amount of your choosing until the line of credit is exhausted.
- **Modified Tenure**- combination of line of credit and scheduled monthly payments for as long as you remain in the home.
- **Modified Term**- combination of line of credit plus monthly payments for a fixed period of months selected by the borrower.

10. What if I change my mind and no longer want the loan after I go to closing? How do I do this?

By law, you have three calendar days to change your mind and cancel the loan. This is called a three day right of rescission. The process of canceling the loan should be explained at loan closing. Be sure to ask the lender for instructions on this process. Mortgage lenders differ in the process of canceling a loan. You should ask for the names of the appropriate people, phone numbers, fax numbers, addresses, or written instructions on whatever process the company has in place. In most cases, the right of rescission will not be applicable to HECM for purchase transactions.

SOCIAL SECURITY

Spouse Benefit

- As a spouse, you can claim a social security benefit based on your own earnings record, or you can collect a spousal benefit that will provide you 50% of the amount of your spouse's social security benefit.

- You are automatically entitled to receive the benefit that provides you the higher monthly amount; either a benefit based on your own earnings, or the spousal benefit, and prior to reaching full retirement age, social security makes this determination for you.

- After you reach full retirement age, you can choose to receive only the spouse's benefit, and delay receiving your retirement benefits until a later date, allowing you to receive a higher benefit later based on the effect of delayed retirement credits. For more information, go to: https://www.socialsecurity.gov/retire 2/delayret.htm.

- You must be age 62 to qualify for either type of social security benefit.

- You cannot collect a spousal benefit until your spouse files for their own benefit.

Spouse Benefit and Early Retirement

- If you collect a spousal benefit, and you begin collecting this benefit before you reach full retirement age, your benefit will be permanently reduced. To see how this reduction is calculated visit the **Benefits for Spouses** section of the social security website at: http://www.ssa.gov/OACT/quickcalc/spouse.html.

- If your spouse takes social security early, and you take a spousal benefit early, you will be significantly reducing the amount of benefits that may be paid out over your lifetime.

Social Security Benefits Upon the Death of a Spouse

- If you are a widow or widower you can collect a survivor's benefit as early as age 60. See the widow/widowers section of the social security website for additional information on how this works: https://www.socialsecurity.gov/survivorplan/survivorchartred.htm

- Once you and your spouse are receiving social security benefits, upon the death of your spouse, you will continue to receive the larger of your benefit, or your spouse's, but not both. This means if you have a longer life expectancy, and you are collecting a benefit based on your spouse's earnings, if your spouse starts taking social security early, it will result in a significant reduction in your benefit too, and the reduction will last throughout your life expectancy.

- A surviving spouse living in the same household is eligible to receive a one-time lump sum payment of $255 upon the death of their spouse.

Divorce – Social Security Benefits (http://www.ssa.gov/retire2/divspouse.htm)

If you are divorced, but your marriage lasted 10 years or longer, you can receive benefits on your ex-spouse's record (even if he or she has remarried). You must also meet the following criteria:

- You are currently unmarried.

- You are at least age 62.

(There are exceptions to the criteria above if your ex-spouse is deceased.) If you collect benefits based on your ex-spouse's record, it will not reduce or affect their benefit in any way. If your ex-spouse has not applied for retirement benefits, but can qualify for them, you may still apply as long as you meet the other criteria, and have been divorced for at least two years.

TAXES

What is the federal Income tax filing status of the surviving spouse after the death of a spouse?

If your spouse died during the year, you are considered married for the whole year for filing purposes.

If you did not remarry before the end of the tax year, you can file a joint return for yourself and your deceased spouse. For the next two years, you may be entitled to the special benefits under Qualifying Widow (er) With Dependent Child. After those two years, you may qualify for Head of Household status.

If you remarried before the end of the tax year, you can file a joint return with your new spouse. Your deceased spouse's filing status is married filing separately for that tax year.

See IRS Publication 501 for more details.

TRUSTS

Revocable Versus Irrevocable Trusts
When it comes to understanding trusts, knowing the difference between revocable and irrevocable trusts is crucial. If you want for a revocable trust and wind up with an irrevocable one, or vice versa, the legal and tax consequences can be significant.

Revocable Living Trusts

A **revocable living trust**, also called a **revocable trust** or **living trust**, is simply a type of trust that can be changed at any time. In other words, if you have second thoughts about a provision in the trust or change your mind about a trust beneficiary or fiduciary, then you can modify the terms of the trust through what's called a trust amendment. Or, if you decide that you don't like anything about the trust at all, then you can either revoke the entire agreement or change the entire contents through an amendment and restatement.

Since revocable living trusts are so flexible, why aren't all trusts revocable? The down side to a revocable trust is that assets funded into the trust will still be considered your own personal assets for creditor and estate tax purposes. This means that a revocable trust offers no creditor protection if you're sued and all assets held in the name of the trust at the time of your death will be subject to both state and federal estate taxes. So why use a revocable living trust as part of your estate plan? For three reasons:

1.   **To plan for mental disability** - Assets held in the name of a revocable living trust at the time a person becomes mentally incapacitated can be managed by their **Disability Trustee** instead of by a court-supervised guardian or conservator.

2.   **To avoid probate** - Assets held in the name of a revocable living trust at the time of a person's death will pass directly to the beneficiaries named in the trust agreement and outside of the probate process.

3.   **To protect the privacy of your property and beneficiaries after you die** - By avoiding probate with a revocable living trust, your trust agreement won't become a public record for the world to see and read. This will keep the details about your assets and who you've decided to leave your estate to a private family matter. Contrast this with a Last Will and Testament that's been admitted to probate - it becomes a public court record that anyone can read.

Irrevocable Trusts

An **irrevocable trust** is simply a type of trust that can't be changed after the agreement has been signed, or a revocable trust that by its design becomes irrevocable after the Trustmaker dies.

With the typical revocable living trust, it will become irrevocable when the Trustmaker dies and can be designed to break into separate irrevocable trusts for the benefit of a surviving spouse, such as with the use of **AB Trusts** or

ABC Trusts, or into multiple irrevocable lifetime trusts for the benefit of children or other beneficiaries. Irrevocable trusts can take on many forms and be used to accomplish a variety of estate planning goals:

•   **Estate Tax Reduction**

   Irrevocable Trusts, such as **irrevocable life insurance trusts (ILIT)**, are commonly used to remove the value of property from a person's estate so that the property can't be taxed when the person dies. In other words, the person who transfers assets into an irrevocable trust is giving over those assets to the trustee and beneficiaries of the trust so that the person no longer owns the assets. Thus, if the person no longer owns the assets, then they can't be taxed when the person later dies.

   As mentioned above, AB Trusts that are created for the benefit of a surviving spouse are irrevocable and, thus, can make full use of the deceased spouse's exemption from estate taxes through the funding of the B Trust with property valued at or below the estate tax exemption. Then, if the value of the deceased spouse's estate exceeds the estate tax exemption, the A Trust will be funded for the benefit of the surviving spouse and payment of estate taxes will be deferred until after the surviving spouse dies.

   ABC Trusts can be used by married couples who live in some of the states that collect a state estate tax and the state estate tax exemption is less than the federal estate tax exemption. For example, in Maryland the state estate tax exemption is only $1 million, as compared with the current federal $5 million exemption, so in Maryland the first $1 million will go into the B

Trust, then next $4 million will go into the C Trust, and anything over $5 million will go into the A Trust.

- **Asset Protection**

Another common use for an irrevocable trust is to provide asset protection for the Trustmaker and the Trustmaker's family. This works in the same way that an irrevocable trust can be used to reduce estate taxes - by placing assets into an irrevocable trust, the Trustmaker is giving up complete control over, and access to, the trust assets and, therefore, the trust assets can't be reached by a creditor of the Trustmaker. However, the Trustmaker's family can be the beneficiaries of the irrevocable trust, thereby still providing the family with financial support, but outside of the reach of creditors. There are also irrevocable trusts called **Self-Settled Trusts** or **Domestic Asset Protection Trusts** that in some states, including Alaska, Delaware, Nevada, and Tennessee, offer creditor protection and allow the Trustmaker to be a trust beneficiary.

In addition, as mentioned above, the various irrevocable trusts that can be created for the benefit of the Trustmaker's surviving spouse or other beneficiaries after the Trustmaker of a revocable living trust dies can be designed to offer asset protection for the trust beneficiaries.

- **Charitable Estate Planning**

Another common use of an irrevocable trust is to accomplish charitable estate planning, such as through a Charitable Remainder Trust or a Charitable Lead Trust. If the Trustmaker makes the initial transfer of assets into a charitable trust while still alive, then the Trustmaker will receive a charitable income tax deduction in the year of the transfer is made. Or, if the initial transfer of assets into a charitable trust doesn't occur until after the Trustmaker's death, then the Trustmaker's estate will receive a charitable estate tax deduction.

AB Trusts and Portability of the Estate Tax Exemption

In 2011 and 2012 the federal estate tax exemption has been made transferable between spouses. This is referred to as "portability of the estate tax exemption" and means that if one spouse dies in 2011 or 2012 and his or her entire $5,000,000 estate tax exemption is not needed to avoid estate taxes on his or her estate, then the unused portion of the deceased spouse's estate tax exemption can be added to the surviving spouse's estate tax exemption. This, in essence, means that a married couple will be able to pass on up to $10,000,000 to their heirs free from federal estate taxes without the need to use AB Trust planning. But keep in mind that if the married couple have different sets of final beneficiaries, such as in the case of a second or later marriage where each spouse has their own children that they want inherit their separate assets after both spouses are deceased, then the couple will want to make use of AB Trust planning in order to insure that their separate beneficiaries will be their ultimate beneficiaries. See glossary for definition of A (Martial) and B (Family) Trusts.

How AB Trust Planning Works

A SENSE OF COMFORT

For You And Your Loved Ones

Here is how the AB Trust system works to maximize the use of both spouses' estate tax exemptions:

1.   **The couple includes the appropriate AB Trust language in their Last Will and Testaments or Revocable Living Trusts.** Note that this should not be attempted without the assistance of a qualified estate planning attorney.

2.   **The couple divides their assets so that each spouse has about the same value of assets in his or her individual name or in his or her Revocable Living Trust.** This is an important step and must be done in order for the AB Trust system to work. Many times couples leave their assets in joint accounts and this completely voids the use of the AB Trust system since the joint assets will pass outright to the surviving spouse instead of through the deceased spouse's Last Will or Revocable Living Trust.

3.   **If the first spouse dies in 2010, 2011 or 2012, then the first $5,000,000 of his or her assets will be funded into the B Trust.** This effectively uses the first spouse's $5,000,000 federal exemption from estate taxes that is available for deaths occurring during these years. The B Trust can be relatively flexible and used for the benefit of the surviving spouse and descendants or other beneficiaries.

4.   **If the deceased spouse's assets exceed $5,000,000, then the excess is funded into the A Trust.** This will defer the payment of estate taxes on the assets above the deceased spouse's $5,000,000 exemption until after the surviving spouse's death. Because of this estate tax deferment, the A Trust is less flexible and can only be used for the benefit of the surviving spouse. In addition, the surviving spouse is required to receive all of the income from the A Trust.

5.   **When the surviving spouse later dies, the surviving spouse will still have his or her own estate tax exemption.** If the exemption is $5,000,000 when the surviving spouse dies, then the first $5,000,000 of the surviving spouse's separate assets will pass estate tax free to the final beneficiaries. Anything over $5,000,000 will be taxed.

6.   **The assets remaining in the B Trust pass estate tax free to the final beneficiaries.** This is because the B Trust used up the $5,000,000 exemption of the first spouse to die, so anything left in the B Trust will pass estate tax free. This can provide a significant windfall to the final beneficiaries if the surviving spouse doesn't need to use the assets from the B Trust and they continue to grow in value during the surviving spouse's remaining lifetime.

The assets remaining in the **A Trust** will be taxed as part of the surviving spouse's estate. As mentioned above, the estate tax on the A Trust is effectively deferred until after the surviving spouse dies.

The balance of the A Trust that remains after the estate tax bill is paid passes to the final beneficiaries. *Note that the beneficiaries of the A and B Trusts can be different.*

As illustrated above, effective use of the AB Trust system allows married couples to pass on up to $10,000,000 to their final beneficiaries, free from any federal estate taxes. AB Trust planning also allows married couples to minimize estate taxes while insuring that the their separate estates will ultimately pass to the beneficiaries of their choice and in the manner of their choice.

What Happens if the A Trust is Not Needed? Enter Portability of the Estate Tax Exemption

What happens if the value of the deceased spouse's estate is under $5,000,000 so that there is no need to establish and fund the A Trust? Then for the 2011 and 2012 tax years, the unused portion of the deceased spouse's estate tax exemption can be transferred and added to the surviving spouse's estate tax exemption. This will be important for couples who have lopsided estates (for example, a second or later marriage where one spouse is wealthier than the other) or where the surviving spouse's estate increases significantly in value after the first spouse's death.

GLOSSARY

5-YEAR RULE	Any earnings distribution prior to the first day of the fifth year after your first Roth was established will be taxed as ordinary income, at whatever your tax rate is at the time.
ADMINISTRATOR ADMINISTRATRIX	A person appointed by the court to administer an *intestate* estate. *Administrator* is the masculine form and *Administratrix* is the feminine form.
ADVANCED MEDICAL DIRECTIVE	Also referred to as a Health Care Power of Attorney, it allows you to appoint a substitute decision maker or agent to make health-care decisions for you if a physician determines that you are incapable of making an informed decision. Your selected agent may refuse to terminate treatment for you when you are either terminal or in a non-terminal state (e.g., persistent vegetative state or coma).
BASIS	The taxpayer's investment in property. The original basis in property is usually the taxpayer's cost. The basis will include payments made to acquire the property, such as commissions, advertising, and legal fees. Basis is adjusted downward when a taxpayer takes depreciation deductions, and basis is adjusted upward when the taxpayer makes improvements.
CARRYOVER BASIS	The basis in property acquired by gift because the donor's basis is carried over to the donee.
CHILDREN'S TRUST	A document that controls when your children will be able to access the money you've left them. Frequently the trust provides for equitable payment of college costs for each child. Then assets are distributed as you direct. Many times parents will choose to stagger when the money is paid out. For example: N at age 25, N at age 30, and the final N at age 40.

COMMUNITY PROPERTY	The ownership interest of the husband and wife in any property acquired by the couple during their marriage in any of the 10 community-property states: Alaska, Arizona, California, Idaho, Louisiana, Nevada, New Mexico, Texas, Washington, and Wisconsin. Unlike *joint tenancy with rights of survivorship* and *tenancy by the entirety*, there is no right of survivorship in community property.
DECEDENT	A deceased person. In the probate context, this term is used to refer to the person whose estate is being administered.
DOMESTIC ASSET PROTECTION TRUSTS	Several states have changed their laws to provide that a person may create a self-settled spendthrift trust (i.e., a spendthrift trust for his or her own benefit). Such trusts are also called Domestic Asset Protection Trusts (DAPT), and sometimes informally called "Alaska trusts", as Alaska was a pioneer in allowing this kind of spendthrift trust. However, because of the danger of the misuse of Alaska trusts to defraud creditors, the legality of such trusts (to the extent that they purport to protect the trust share of a beneficiary who is also a creator of the trust) is uncertain in the states not allowing self-settled spendthrift trusts. Nevada has enacted a series of statutes, codified at Chapter 166 of the Nevada Revised Statutes that specifically enable the creation of self-settled spendthrift trusts. This form of trust is commonly referred to as a "Nevada Asset Protection Trust". Under Chapter 166, an individual can serve as the settlor, trustee and beneficiary of the trust. The following other states now have a DAPT statute: Delaware, South Dakota, Wyoming, Tennessee, Utah, Oklahoma, Colorado, Missouri, Rhode Island and New Hampshire.
DURABLE GENERAL FINANCIAL POWER OF ATTORNEY	A document that establishes who will act on your behalf (your 'agent') in financial matters if you are incapacitated. The agent can manage your assets, sign a tax return, pay your bills, or even sell property. He or she can also fund a "living trust." Many banks, other financial institutions, and brokerages are increasingly hesitant to accept this document. In addition, you may want to also sign the bank's, other financial institution's, and brokerage house's power of attorney form as a safeguard to ensure that the institution will allow your selected agent to act for you. The Durable General Financial Power of Attorney is automatically revoked upon your death.
ETHICAL WILLS	An ethical will is a document written to communicate values and wisdom, history, stories, and love from one generation to another. It preserves who you are and what matters most to you. It's a way for you to be remembered and to make a real difference. This writing is spiritual in nature. They differ from your will of "valuables," a legal declaration assigning the inheritors your

	property and material "stuff". Ethical wills are **not** legal documents. Examples of Ethical Will can be found at: http://www.ethicalwill.com/examples.html
EXECUTOR / EXECUTRIX	A person appointed by a *testator* to administer a *testate* estate. That person should be sensitive to the needs of your beneficiaries, competent to handle financial and legal matters, and available and willing to take on responsibilities. *Executor* is the masculine form and *Executrix* is the feminine form.
FAMILY TRUST	Also known as a *B trust* or a *credit equivalent trust*, the family trust is funded with up to the maximum assets that can pass with no tax due (currently $5 million). These assets are taxed at death, but because each person has a unified credit, no tax is actually due. Once these assets have been taxed (with no tax due), they are free to grow to any amount and will never be taxed again for estate purposes.
GIFT TAX ANNUAL EXCLUSION	Allows a person to make gifts of a present interest up to $13,000 per donee, without gift tax consequences. Can be used with any number of donees. The annual exclusion amount will be indexed for inflation, but indexing will only increase the exclusion in increments of $1,000.
GIFT-SPLITTING	Is permitted with a spouse under gift tax rules, but not under estate tax rules. Under gift-splitting, the annual exclusion is in effect, enlarged to $26,000 per donee for married persons. The spouse must consent to gift-splitting, and a federal gift tax return must be filed reflecting the election to split gifts.
GROSS ESTATE	The Gross Estate of the decedent consists of an accounting of everything you own or have certain interests in at the date of death. (See IRS publication 950) The fair market value of these items is used, not necessarily what you paid for them or what their values were when you acquired them. The total of all of these items is your "Gross Estate." The includible property may consist of cash and securities, real estate, insurance, trusts, annuities, business interests and other assets. Keep in mind that the Gross Estate will likely include non-probate as well as probate property.
GUARDIAN	The person(s) who will oversee care and custody of your minor children or disabled individuals and administer their assets. They should know your children already (if possible), be consulted in advance, have similar philosophic views to your own, and be financially able to take on the responsibility of caring for your children.

INHERITED IRA	An IRA that passes to a beneficiary at the death of the IRA owner. If you name your spouse as the beneficiary of your IRA, your spouse inherits the IRA at your death. At that point, it is your spouse's property. But if you name anyone other than your spouse, that beneficiary inherits the rights to income from your IRA, which continues to be registered in your name, but not the IRA itself. All inherited IRAs are subject to annual IRS required minimum distribution (RMD) rules, but these are generally based on the inheritor's own life expectancy. This enables continued investment in an Inherited IRA without the impact of immediate taxes, so that you can potentially maximize these inherited assets.
INTER VIVOS	The legal term *inter vivos* is a Latin phrase meaning "between the living." An inter vivos gift is a transfer of property from one person to another during the lifetime of the original property holder (as opposed to a *testamentary* transfer, which takes effect at death only). An inter vivos trust (also called a living trust) is a trust that takes effect during lifetime (as opposed to testamentary trusts, which take effect at death only).
INTESTATE	A term used to describe a person, estate, or portion of an estate for which there is no valid Last Will and Testament. The estate of a person who dies without a will is distributed according to state law, called *intestate law* or *laws of intestacy*.
IRREVOCABLE LIFE INSURANCE TRUST	A document that removes the value of your life insurance from your taxable estate. You irrevocably assign your policies to the trust. This means you can't change your beneficiaries at a later date. You choose a trustee to make sure the policy premiums are paid. If you transfer life insurance policies to an irrevocable trust, you must live three years past the date of transfer or the value of the policies will be pulled back into your estate.
IRREVOCABLE TRUSTS	A trust that can't be modified or terminated without the permission of the beneficiary. The grantor, having transferred assets into the trust, effectively removes all of his or her rights of ownership to the assets and the trust. The main reason for setting up an irrevocable trust is for estate and tax considerations. The benefit of this type of trust for estate assets is that it removes all incidents of ownership, effectively removing the trust's assets from the grantor's taxable estate. The grantor is also relieved of the tax liability on the income generated by the assets. While the tax rules will vary between jurisdictions, in most cases, the grantor can't receive these benefits if he or she is the trustee of the trust.
JOINT TENANCY WITH RIGHTS OF SURVIVORSHIP	Each joint tenant has an equal ownership interest in the property. The joint tenants acquire the same interest in the same property at the same time, and they take possession simultaneously.

	Ownership of the property passes by operation of law to the surviving tenants. The ownership interest of tenants who die, passes outside of probate and is not subject to testamentary disposition. During the joint tenant's lifetime, the interest can be sold or disposed of by converting the joint tenancy to a tenancy in common.
LIVING WILL	Declares your desire that life-sustaining treatment be withdrawn or withheld under certain specific medical conditions. A Living Will may apply to cases where an individual is terminally ill or in a persistent vegetative state. A Living Will may also declare your desire that life-sustaining treatment be continued.
MARTIAL TRUST	Also known as an "A" trust, the marital trust provides management for assets passed to your spouse. (The alternative is to leave assets for your spouse outright—no trust.) If no restrictions are placed on what happens to the assets when the second spouse dies, it's called a "general power of appointment." If you choose to control what happens upon the death of your spouse, you need to establish a Qualified Terminable Interest Property Trust or "QTIP" Trust (a stricter form of marital trust).
PERSONAL REPRESENTATIVE	A term some jurisdictions use to refer a person appointed to administer an estate.
PROBATE	A court process that makes sure that all your final debts are paid and that your Will is executed. It is the process which allows for the transfer of assets from a deceased person to his or her intended beneficiaries. All assets that require your signature to be transferred will be probated and thus under Court control. These include: all assets titled in your name individually; all assets held as tenants-in-common (as opposed to joint-tenants-with-rights-of-survivorship or tenants by the entirety); and all benefits that are payable to your estate. Probate can be a lengthy and costly process.
PROBATE ESTATE	The probate estate is the assets or liabilities of a deceased person that are subject to the court-supervised probate process. Not every asset a person owns when he or she dies is included in his or her probate estate. The following are examples of property not included in the probate estate and are not subjected to the probate process: Jointly owned property, assets held in trust, life insurance (where the designated beneficiary is not the deceased's estate), pay on death (POD) accounts which specified a beneficiary, social security survivor's benefits, retirement accounts (where the designated beneficiary is not the deceased's estate), Veterans benefits, employee benefits property given away before death.

QUALIFIED DOMESTIC TRUST (QDOT)	A type of trust that can be set up for the benefit of a non-U.S. citizen spouse to help defer estate taxes to a future date.
QUALIFIED TERMINABLE INTEREST PROPERTY (QTIP) TRUST	Often used in second marriages in which children are involved, a QTIP trust allows the creator of the trust to determine where his or her assets will ultimately go after the spouse dies.
REQUIRED MINIMUM DISTRIBUTION	Required Minimum Distributions (RMDs) generally are minimum amounts that a retirement plan account owner must withdraw annually starting with the year that he or she reaches 70 ½ years of age or, if later, the year in which he or she retires. However, if the retirement plan account is an IRA or the account owner is a 5% owner of the business sponsoring the retirement plan, the RMDs must begin once the account holder is age 70 ½, regardless of whether he or she is retired. The RMD rules also apply to Roth 401k accounts. However, the RMD rules do not apply to Roth IRAs while the account owner is alive. Retirement plan participants and IRA owners are responsible for taking the correct amount of RMDs on time every year from their accounts, and they face stiff penalties for failure to take RMDs. When a retirement plan account owner or IRA owner dies before RMDs have begun, different RMD rules apply to the beneficiary of the account or IRA. Generally, the entire amount of the owner's benefit must be distributed to the beneficiary who is an individual either (1) within 5 years of the owner's death, or (2) over the life of the beneficiary starting no later than one year following the owner's death.
RETIRED SERVICEMAN'S FAMILY PROTECTION PLAN (RSFPP)	If entitled to military retirement pay before September 21, 1972, the retiree had the chance to elect to a RSFPP annuity for his/her surviving spouse. The Survivor Benefit Plan (SBP) replaced RSFPP on September 21, 1972, making RSFPP unavailable to those qualifying for retired pay after that date.
RETIREMENT PLANS	**403(b) Retirement Plans: A 403(b)** plan is a U.S. tax-advantaged retirement savings plan available for public education organizations, some non-profit employers (only Internal Revenue Code 501(c)(3) organizations), cooperative hospital service organizations, and self-employed ministers in the United States. It has tax treatment similar to a 401(k) plan, especially after the Economic Growth and Tax Relief Reconciliation Act of 2001. Employee salary deferrals into a 403(b) plan are made before income tax is paid and allowed to grow tax-deferred until the money is taxed as income when withdrawn from the plan. 403(b) plans are also referred to as a tax-sheltered annuity although since 1974 they no longer are restricted to an annuity form and participants can also invest in mutual funds. **457 Retirement Plans:** The **457 plan** is a type of non-qualified

	tax advantaged deferred-compensation retirement plan that is available for governmental and certain non-governmental employers in the United States. The employer provides the plan and the employee defers compensation into it on a pre-tax basis. For the most part the plan operates similarly to a 401(k) or 403(b) plan most people are familiar with in the US. The key difference is that unlike with a 401(k) plan, there is no 10% penalty for withdrawal before the age of 59½ (although the withdrawal is subject to ordinary income taxation). Also 457 plans (both governmental and non-governmental) can allow independent contractors to participate in the plan where 401(k) and 403(b) plans cannot.
REVERSE MORTGAGE	A form of equity release (or lifetime mortgage) available in the United States. It is a loan available to seniors aged 62 or older, under a Federal program administered by the Department of Housing and Urban Development (HUD). It enables eligible homeowners to access a portion of their equity. The homeowners can draw the mortgage principal in a lump sum, by receiving monthly payments over a specified term or over their (joint) lifetimes, as a revolving line of credit, or some combination thereof. The homeowners' obligation to repay the loan is deferred until owner (or survivor of two) dies, the home is sold, they cease to live in the property, or they breach the provisions of the mortgage (such as failure to maintain the property in good repair, pay property taxes, and keep the property insured against fire, etc.). The owner can be out of the home for up to 364 consecutive days (i.e., into aged care). At that time, the estate has approximately 6 months to repay the balance of the reverse mortgage or sell the home to pay off the balance. All remaining equity is inherited by the estate. The estate is not personally liable if the home sells for less than the balance of the reverse mortgage.
REVOCABLE TRUSTS	The Grantor retains full and absolute control over the Revocable Trust and its asset, and can amend or revoke it at any time. A Revocable Trust also acts like a Will when the Grantor dies. Upon the Grantor's death, the successor Trustee distributes the assts to the intended beneficiaries, either outright or in trust. Assets titled in the name of the Revocable Trust are not subjected to the probate process upon death, which saves time and money. It is like a power of attorney to allow for the management of the Revocable Trust assets upon the Grantor's incapacity. It is also more difficult to contest than a Will.
SECONDARY INSURANCE COMPANY	An insurance company that fills the void of unpaid amounts left by a policyholder's primary insurer.

SECONDARY POLICY HOLDER	A person who is entitled to benefits of an insurance policy held by the primary policy holder.
SELF-SETTLED TRUSTS	A trust created by an individual for his or her own benefit is sometimes called a "self-settled trust", and may be a kind of asset-protection trust. If the creator of a self-settled trust is also a beneficiary of the trust, a particular problem in the context of protection of creditors and prevention of fraud is presented: the danger that the creator of the trust is trying to defraud creditors. To prevent individuals from creating trusts to defeat their own creditors, the laws of most states provide that a spendthrift clause in a trust document does not protect the beneficiary to the extent that the beneficiary is also the person who created the trust. The settlor does not need to be either the sole settlor or the only beneficiary of the trust. As long as the settlor is a beneficiary of the trust to any extent, to that extent the trust will be deemed self-settled.
SETTLOR / GRANTOR	Settlor/Grantor: In law a settlor is a person who settles property on trust law for the benefit of beneficiaries. In some legal systems, a settlor is also referred to as a trustor, or occasionally, a grantor or donor. Where the trust is a testamentary trust, the settlor is usually referred to as the testator. The settlor may also be the trustee of the trust (where he declares that he holds his own property on trusts) or a third party may be the trustee (where he transfers the property to the trustee on trusts).
SPECIAL NEEDS TRUST	A trust that can be set up for a disabled person. By specifying that assets are only to be used for luxuries and not basic care, the trust allows the disabled person continued eligibility for government financial aid.
SPENDTHRIFT TRUSTS	A type of trust that is overseen by a trustee such as a bank or a private lender. The trustee controls the how the assets are distributed to the beneficiary after the trust creator has become deceased or incapacitated. The beneficiary is usually not allowed to spend the money before they actually receive distributions from the trust fund. In a spendthrift trust, the beneficiary is sometimes referred to as the "spendthrift". Spendthrift literally means a person who wastes away their financial estate through imprudent living or excessive spending. However, the beneficiary is not actually required to have a history of bad spending in order to be named in the spendthrift trust.

STEP–UP IN BASIS	Those assets included in the taxable estate of a decedent and distributed by the estate receive a step-up in basis. The receivers of these bequests receive a basis in those assets equal to the fair market value at the date of death or, alternatively, six months after death. *Step-Up in basis does not apply to retirement accounts* (401k, regular and Roth IRAs, etc).
SUCCESSOR TRUSTEE	An individual who manages and controls a trust after its trustee dies or is incapacitated. For example, the person who creates a trust, called a grantor, may be his own trustee, managing and controlling the trust's assets. He may appoint another person to be a successor trustee, managing the assets when he is no longer able to do so. While the successor trustee cannot use the trust's assets to his own benefit, unless he is also a beneficiary of the trust, he can sell, transfer, and distribute assets according to the instructions the grantor created for the trust.
SURVIVOR BENEFIT PLAN (SBP)	Retired military pay stops when the veteran dies. SBP helps make up for the loss of part of this income. It pays the veteran's eligible survivors an inflation-adjusted monthly income. The veteran must pay premiums for SBP coverage once you retire. Premiums are taken by reducing retired pay, so they don't count as income. This means less tax and less out-of-pocket cost for SBP. Also, using conservative fiscal assumptions, the overall plan is partially funded by the government, so the average premiums are well below cost. This subsidy means an attractive plan for most people. The subsidy is an average and should not be considered to apply in every case. Basic SBP for a spouse pays a benefit equal to 55 percent of the veteran's retired pay. Eligible children may also be SBP beneficiaries, either alone or added to spouse coverage. In the latter case, the children get benefits only if the spouse dies or remarries before age 55. Eligible children equally divide a benefit equal to 55 percent of your retired pay. Child coverage is relatively inexpensive because children get benefits only while they are still the veteran's dependents. The veteran may choose coverage for a former spouse or, if he/she has no spouse or children, the veteran may be able to cover an "insurable interest" (such as, a business partner or parent).
TAXABLE ESTATE	The total assets that will be taxed at your death. To determine whether your estate will be subject to estate tax, add up all of your assets plus your home (50% if owned as joint tenants) and life insurance and subtract any of the following: unified credit, unlimited marital deduction, and unlimited charitable deduction. Whatever is left is your taxable estate.

TENANTS BY THE ENTIRETY	Is joint tenancy ownership of property by spouses. When a spouse dies, the surviving spouse becomes the sole owner of the property by operation of law. The sale or transfer of the entireties property requires the consent of both spouses. As such, this property is not subject to the creditors of an individual spouse.
TENANTS IN COMMON	Property is held in tenancy in common when two or more persons own an undivided, fractional interest in the property. The fractional interests may be unequal. Each co-tenant owns a portion of the property separately and can transfer that interest at any time, without the consent of the other co-tenants. Each co-tenant has testamentary control over his or her share of the property, and the fractional interest is included in the deceased owner's probate estate and in his or her gross estate.
TESTAMENTARY	A term used to describe a relation to a Last Will and Testament. For example, *testamentary intent* refers to the intent needed to make a Will. *Testamentary gifts* or *testamentary transfers* refer to gifts or transfers that take place at death (in contrast with *inter vivos* gifts or transfers, which take place during life). A *testamentary trust* is a trust that takes effect at a person's death (in contrast to an *inter vivos* (living) trust that takes effect during life.
TESTATOR / TESTATRIX	A person who makes a Will. Testator is the masculine form and Testatrix is the feminine form.
THRIFT SAVINGS PLAN (TSP)	The Thrift Savings Plan (TSP) is a retirement savings and investment plan for Federal employees and members of the uniformed services, including the Ready Reserve. It was established by Congress in the Federal Employees' Retirement System Act of 1986 and offers the same types of savings and tax benefits that many private corporations offer their employees under 401(k) plans. The TSP is a defined contribution plan, meaning that the retirement income you receive from your TSP account will depend on how much you (and your agency, if you are eligible to receive agency contributions) put into your account during your working years and the earnings accumulated over that time.
TRANSFER ON DEATH (TOD) OR PAYABLE ON DEATH (POD)	A type of non-retirement account that allows you to name a beneficiary just like you would on an IRA or other type of retirement account. At death, your assets flow directly to your beneficiaries without going through probate.
TRUSTEE	A person who holds title to assets that will be used for the benefit of someone else. When choosing a trustee for your trust, look for someone who is financially capable, responsible, and sensitive to your family's needs.

TRUSTS	Is an arrangement created by a Grantor or Settlor where a Trustee administers and invests assets for the benefit of beneficiaries. Trusts can either be revocable or irrevocable. Trusts can be created during your lifetime (living or inter vivos trusts) or upon death (testamentary trusts).
UNIFIED CREDIT	A credit for a portion of estate tax due on taxable estates. Everyone is allowed one unified credit. In 2012, the unified credit amount for both estate and gift tax purposes will $1,772,800 (exempting $5,120,000 from tax).
UNLIMITED CHARITABLE DEDUCTION	Allows anyone to bypass estate tax by gifting property to a qualified charity.
UNLIMITED MARTIAL DEDUCTION	Allows one spouse to pass an unlimited amount of assets tax-free to the other spouse in life or at death (unless one spouse is not a U.S. citizen).
WILL	A document that controls the flow of your personal property like jewelry, family heirlooms, and assets held in your name only. It does not control what passes by beneficiary designation (for example, life insurance, IRAs, retirement plans, Transfer on Death agreements), by contract (for example, accounts held by joint tenancy with rights of survivorship), or by trust.

Sources

http://altmanassociates.com/clients-colleagues/client-cherish-letter/

http://en.wikipedia.org/wiki/Reverse_mortgage

http://en.wikipedia.org/wiki/Spendthrift_trust#The_general_rule:_Self settled_trusts_do_not_protect_the_trust_creator

http://ncwillsandtrusts.com/2009/09/8-questions-to-ask-before-hiring-an-estate-planning-lawyer/

http://portal.hud.gov/hudportal/HUD?src=/program_offices/housing/sfh/hecm/rmtopten

http://reversemortgageguides.org/

http://wills.about.com/od/overviewoftrusts/a/abtrust.htm   *By Julie Garber*

http://wills-probate.lawyers.com/wills-probate/

http://www.legacyfuneralcare.com/death-certificates.php

http://www.realpagessites.com/meyerlawfirm/nss-folder/folder/questions-estate-planning-attorney.pd

Keir Educational Resources, Reference Guide for Financial Planners 2012

www.archives.gov

www.caringinfo.org

www.cfp.net

www.federalretirement.net

www.fortenberrylaw.com/glossary/

www.ftc.gov/funerals/

www.funerals.org

www.investopedia.com/terms/q/QTIP.asp

www.irs.gov

www.legalmatch.com

www.life-legacies.com/ethicalwills

www.livingtrustnetwork.com

www.military.com

www.moaa.org

www.morningstar.com

www.naela.org

www.nelf.org

www.nolo.com/legal-encyclopedia/

www.obliviousinvestor.com/inherited-ira-rules/

www.opm.gov

www.organdonor.gov

www.socialsecurity.gov

www.tsp.gov

www.usaa.com

www.va.gov

ADDITIONAL NOTES / INFORMATION:

CPSIA information can be obtained at www.ICGtesting.com
Printed in the USA
BVOW052000190313

315941BV00005B/17/P